The Personal Instructor 7

Mickey Baker's
Complete Handbook For The Music Arranger

© 1972
Amsco Music Publishing Company, New York
Music Sales Limited, London

© 1972 Amsco Music Publishing Company
33 West 60th Street, New York 10023

Music Sales Limited
78 Newman Street
W1E 4JZ London

Library of Congress Card Catalogue Number: 70-113641
International Standard Book Number: 0-8256-2807-5

Contents

Part I Polyphonic Composition, 4
    The Intervals, 5
    The Species, 7
    The Canon, 12
    Melodic Changes of The Theme, 13
    Imitation by Contrary Motion, 14
    The Invention, 15
    Three-Part Polyphony, 21
    Three-Part Canon, 23
    Fugato, 24
    The Stretto, 26
    The Three-Part Invention, 27
    Four-Part Invention, 31
    The Fugue, 34
    The Exposition, 36
    The Remaining Sections, 37
    2, 3, and 5-Voiced Fugues, 40
    Conclusion, 40

Part II Orchestration, 41
    Instrumentation, 42
    The Violin, 42
    The Viola, 44
    The Cello, 45
    The Double Bass, 46
    The Flute in C, 47
    The Flute in G (Alto), 47
    The Piccolo in C, 48
    The Oboe (in C), 48
    The English Horn (Cor Anglais) in F, 49
    The Clarinet (B♭ and A), 49
    The E♭ Clarinet, 50
    The Bass Clarinet (B♭), 51
    The Bassoon, 51
    Contra-Bassoon, 51
    The Horn in F (French Horn), 52
    The Brass (The B♭ Trumpet), 53
    The Trombone (B♭), 53
    The Bass Trombone, 53
    The Tuba, 53
    The Harp, 55
    Percussion Instruments
      with Definite Pitch, 56
    The Kettle Drum, 56
    Chimes, 57
    The Xylophone, 57
    Key Board Percussion, 57
    The Piano, 57
    The Celesta, 57
    Percussion Instruments
      with Indefinite Pitch, 58
    Side-Drum, 58
    Bass Drum, 58
    Triangle, 58
    Cymbals, 59
    Gong, 59
    Tamborine, 59

Part III Voicing, 60
    Part Writing, 61
    Duet Writing, 62
    Trio Writing, 62
    4-Part Writing, 63
    Double Stops on the Violin,
      Viola and Cello, 63
    Three and Four Note Chords, 64

Part IV The String Orchestra, 65
    The Non-Harmonic Elements, 69
    Arpeggio and Pedal Treatment, 72
    Bowings, 73
    Exact Tremolo, 76
    Bowed Tremolo, 77
    The Fingered (Slurred) Tremolo, 77
    Pizzacato, 78
    Other Devices in Use for Strings, 78

Part V Wood-Winds and Horns, 79
    Combination of Trumpets,
      Trombones and Horns, 84

Part VI Full Ensemble, 88
    Suggestions For Scoring, 88
    Melodic Lines in The Middle, 92
    Treatment of a Principal Melodic
      Line in Bass, 93
    Combination of Wood-Winds and Horns, 94
    Wood-Winds, Horns and Strings, 95

Part VII Big Band Arranging, 96
    The Saxophones, 96
    Open Voicing, 100
    Five Saxophones, 100
    Saxophone Trills, 104
    The Brass, 105
    The Rhythm Section, 107
    Ensemble with Concerted Rhythm, 109
    Odd Combinations, 110
    Free Jazz, 112
    Contrapuntal Treatment, 113

Part VIII The Strings With Big Bands, 114
    Strings as Solo, Soli (melody
      or Counter Melody), 114
    Strings and Saxophones, Clarinets,
      Flutes, etc, 115
    Effects, 115

Part IX Symphonic Effects
  in Modern Arranging, 116

Part X Choral Arranging, 124
    Voice Leading, 124
    TBB Combination, 127
    TB Combination, 128
    Female Voices (Treble Voices), 128
    SSA Combination, 128

Part I

POLYPHONIC COMPOSITION

This section is devoted to Polyphony: the Canon, the Invention and the Fugue. Polyphony, which is to say, counterpoint, has many possibilities which have yet to be exploited in commercial music writing. There is a great need for more contrapuntalism in this area, as a relief from the overuse of boring homophonic techniques.

COUNTERPOINT

Counterpoint is polyphony; two or more melodies moving together simultaneously.

LICENSES

It is best to start writing melodies in stepwise motion (Ex. 1 Ⓐ). However, there are no rules as far as movement during the same chord repetition (Ⓑ). A skip to any note may be made downward (or upward) to any note that tends to move upwards and vice versa (Ⓒ).

A downward scale passage may skip upward and continue its downward movement and an upward passage may skip downward, etc. (Ex. 2Ⓐ). A skip in sequences is always good (Ⓑ). Skips in 3rds and 6ths are good (Ⓒ).

By what is known as the deferred resolution, a suspension may leap downward to a note of harmony, then move stepwise into its natural resolution (Ex. 3Ⓐ). Non-harmonic elements may also be introduced (Ⓑ). When moving stepwise to a desired tone it is best to enter the tone by step, not by leap (Ⓒ).

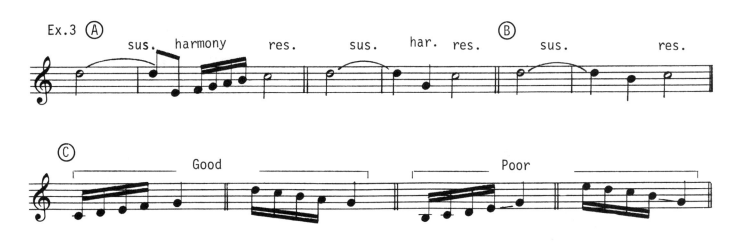

THE INTERVALS

In two part counterpoint there are no parallel perfect 4ths or 5ths and no parallel octaves or unisons (Ex. 4 Ⓐ, Ⓑ, Ⓒ, Ⓓ).

4th, 5th and octaves become possible when in contrary motion (Ex. 5Ⓐ, Ⓑ, Ⓒ, Ⓓ).

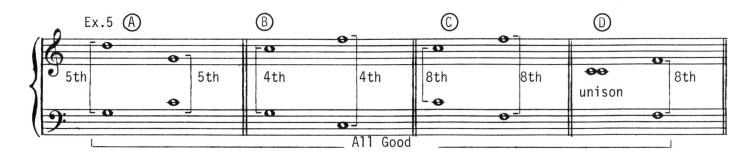

Hidden (open) octaves and 5ths are caused by approaching these perfect intervals with "wide" skips in similar motion (Ex. 6Ⓐ, Ⓑ) but if one of the tones move stepwise the effect is good (Ex. 6Ⓒ, Ⓓ).

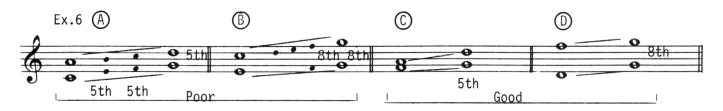

Two dissonant intervals in succession are only possible in stepwise contrary motion (Ex. 7 Ⓐ, Ⓑ). Three stepwise (diatonic) tones may be taken in contrary motion in two part counterpoint (Ex. 7 Ⓒ, Ⓓ).

RESOLUTION OF INTERVALS

Ⓐ: The 2nd expands in contrary or oblique motion. Ⓑ: The 7th contracts in contrary or oblique motion. Ⓒ: The 3rd and 6th need no adjustment. Ⓓ: The 4th and 5th are followed by the 3rd and 6th (Ex. 8 Ⓐ, Ⓑ, Ⓒ, Ⓓ).

Ex.8 Ⓐ

The 2nd may also skip a P4 in one voice.

Assignment

Analyze Ex. 1 through 8 and write similar examples of all the intervals in different major keys.

THE FIRST SPECIES
(Note Against Note)

CANTO FERMO
CANTAS FIRMAS $= $ C. F. $ = $ The "Fixed" song

COUNTERPOINT $ = $ C. P. $ = $ The Melody which is written against the C. F.

A note of C. P. is written against a note of C. F. each note being of *equal constant value* throughout—except possibly at the first and last measures. You should aim at contrary motion and not use more than 3 or 4 parallel 3rds and 6ths. The use of sequences is desirable. Example 9 Ⓐ shows the 1st species in half note against half note $ = $ ♩. Ⓑ shows the 1st species in quarter note against quarter note $ = $ ♩.

Assignment

You are to write similar exercises of Ex. 9 in different major keys. Select any chord cycle of 8 measures and write two parts. Study the text of Ex. 9 and follow this formula. Make 3 or 4 examples of each species and remember that it is note against note 𝄽 or 𝅘𝅥 . You are also to write 𝅘𝅥𝅘𝅥 and 𝅘𝅥𝅯𝅘𝅥𝅯𝅘𝅥𝅯𝅘𝅥𝅯 .

To write counterpoint you must discipline your writing habits and this can only be achieved through constant practice. By writing counterpoint through the species you will soon put all of the examples from 1 through 9 to work (with constant review) and this is *absolutely necessary* if you intend to write inventions and fugues.

N.B. End all of your musical examples with a V, I close, and carefully arrange the movement of the parts.

2ND SPECIES

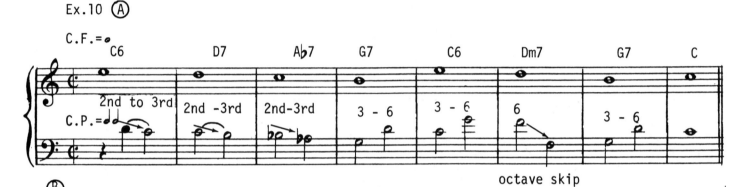

3RD SPECIES

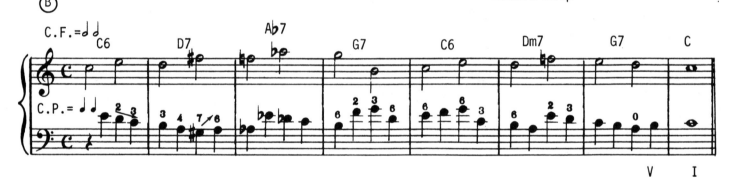

Ex. 12 Ⓐ shows a musical example of C. F. in melody. Ex. 12 Ⓑ shows an example with C. F. in bass. Ex. Ⓒ shows the sequence, but the intervals are *altered* between the *first two notes*. It is always possible to alter a musical passage if it suits the harmonic structure.

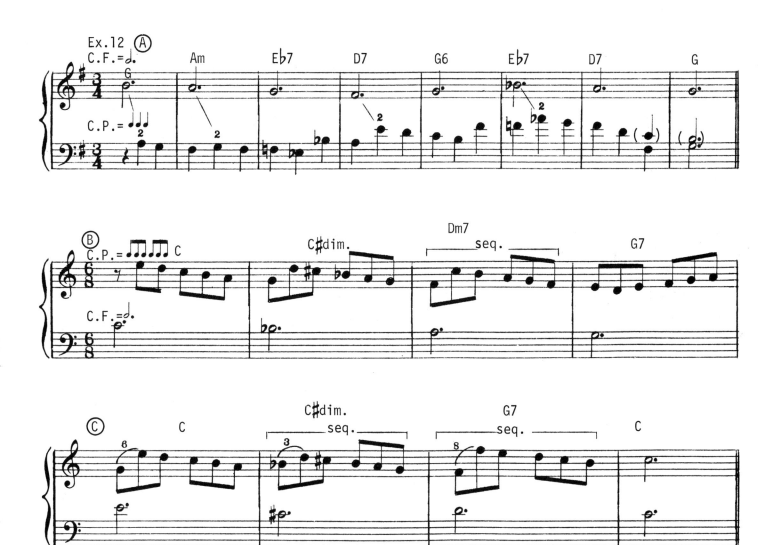

Assignment

Write examples of the 2nd and 3rd species in many different varieties.

4TH SPECIES

This species is the same as the 2nd species, the only difference being that the 2nd note of the measure is tied over, creating a suspension in most cases. Ex. 13Ⓐ. In cases of extreme difficulty the tie may be broken (Ex. 13Ⓑ) and the use of the deferred resolution is used at the final cadence (Ex. 13Ⓒ).

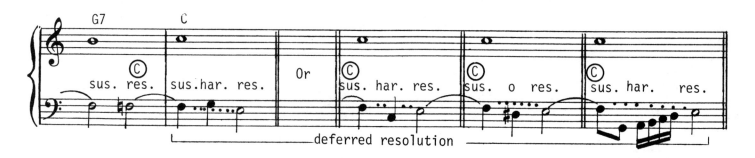

THE 5TH SPECIES
(Florid)

This species is a combination of all the other four species and not merely the succession of the 1st, 2nd, 3rd and 4th. It is a judicious mixture of all of them. Dotted rhythms are allowed; also, rests for variety (Ex. 14).

Ex.14

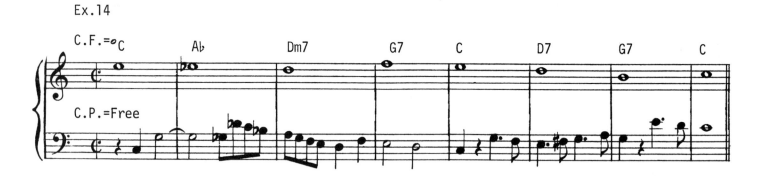

Assignment

Write examples of the 4th species using the suspension and close with a deferred resolution. Write examples of the 5th species as follows: There are 4 two measure examples in Ex. 15; you are to make an 8 measure phrase of each one, using all of the species as indicated (Ex. 15Ⓐ).

Ex. 15Ⓐ C.F. = 𝅗𝅥 𝅗𝅥   Ⓑ C.F. = ♩♩♩♩   Ⓒ C.F. = 𝅗𝅥𝅗𝅥 with suspension   Ⓓ C.F. = 5th species
C.P.   5th species   C.P.   5th species   C.P.   5th species   C.P. = 5th species

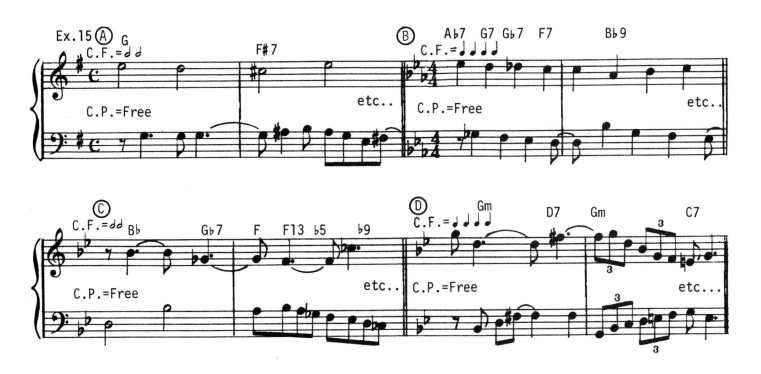

OBBLIGATO
(C. P.)

This type of C. P. is applied to any given melody (or harmony) and it follows all of the normal rules, i.e., the C. P. should satisfy the melody, the harmony and still *maintain its own definite character*. Ex. 16 Ⓐ shows a melody with obbligato C. P. Ex. 16 Ⓑ and Ⓒ show alternate C. P. that could be applied to the same melody (C. F.). They are also above the melody.

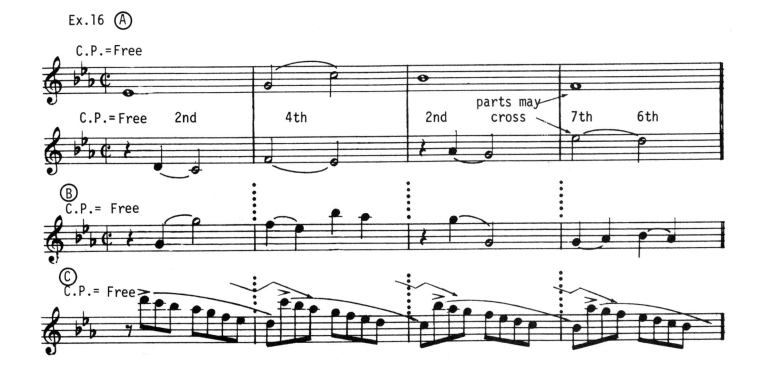

Assignment

Select any type of compositions and write two obbligato C. P.'s to each. This can work well with the popular tunes of today.

THE CANON

The Canon is the strictest form of polyphonic music and it puts into practice continuous imitation. All forms of C. P. (canon, invention, fugue) employ the *imitation technique.* In two part canon the first statement is made by the motive (theme) alone. Then, it is imitated in another voice while the original motive takes up counterpoint (1) and it continues as follows:

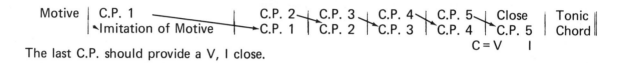

The last C.P. should provide a V, I close.

CANON AT THE OCTAVE

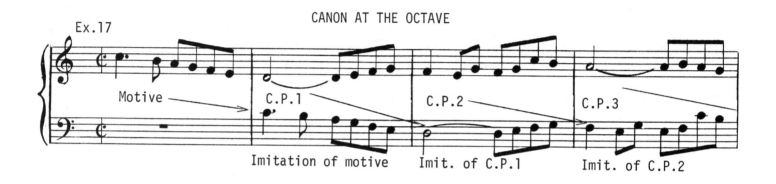

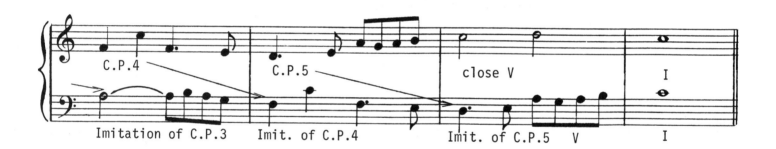

But there is no limit as to how many counterpoints can be used. Ex. 17 shows an 8 measure phrase in canon so at C. P. 5, a V, I close is necessary.

Ex. 17 is a canon imitated at the octave, which means that each imitation is made in the octave. Ex. 18 is a canon imitation in the 2nd. Analyze them carefully.

CANON AT THE 2nd

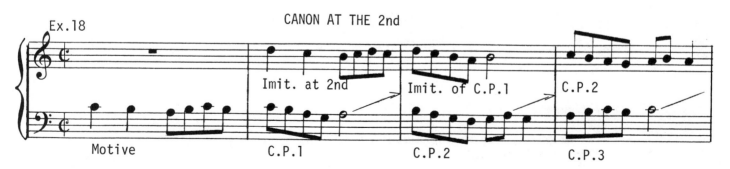

C.P.3   C.P.4   C.P.5   I

C.P.4   C.P.5   close   C= V   I

Assignment

Imitations are possible on every step of the scale. You are to write 8 measure canons on each step. Do not write with chord progression in mind because true polyphonic writing is not written in chord cycles as such.

MELODIC CHANGES OF THE THEME

Melodic changes are made to make the theme (motive) *conform to a harmonic structure* (Ex. 19 Ⓐ). The first or last note of a theme may be enlarged or reduced if it aids the structure (Ⓑ); the theme may be augmented or diminished for variety (Ⓒ); the rhythm may be shifted starting the motive on an accented or unaccented beat (Ⓓ); the quantity of one or more intervals may be augmented or diminished to a 3rd, 4th, 5th, 6th or 7th (Ⓔ). Non-harmonic elements are used to embellish the theme after its first announcement. Analyze Ex. 19 Ⓐ, Ⓑ, Ⓒ, Ⓓ, and Ⓔ. Notice that the same motive is used throughout.

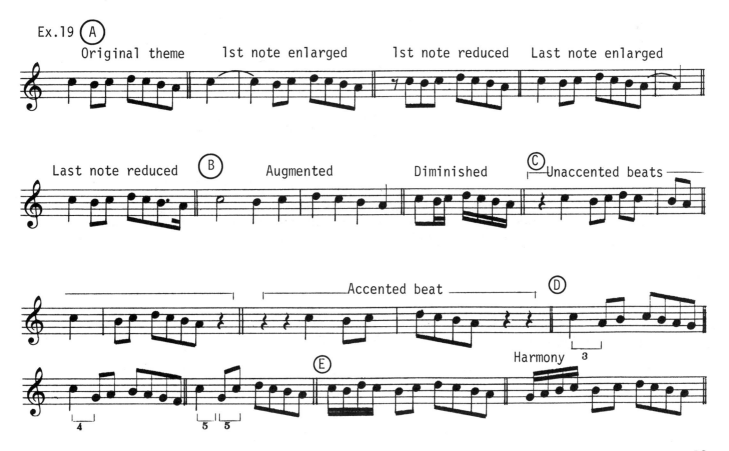

Ex.19 Ⓐ
Original theme   1st note enlarged   1st note reduced   Last note enlarged

Last note reduced   Ⓑ   Augmented   Diminished   Ⓒ Unaccented beats

Accented beat   Ⓓ

Ⓔ   Harmony

IMITATION BY CONTRARY MOTION

Contrary motion means that the motive is written upside down. Mediant to mediant (same as tonic to dominant) contrary motion means that the 3rd appears just as it did in the original motive even though it is upside down (Ex. 20 Ⓐ, Ⓑ). Ex. 20 Ⓒ, Ⓓ shows mediant to tonic in contrary motion. These are the best for contrary motion because of the harmonic relationship.

Ex.20 Ⓐ

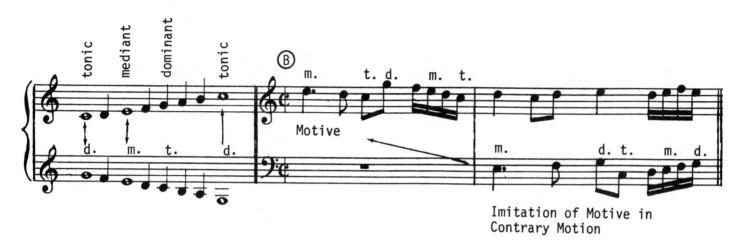

Imitation of Motive in
Contrary Motion

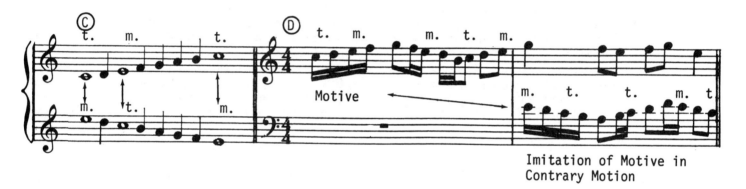

Imitation of Motive in
Contrary Motion

Assignment

All of the foregone material is used in *free imitation*, i.e., in agreeing with the prevailing scale. Write a few one measure motives with the response in contrary motion.

N.B. Complex forms of contrary motion, melodic and rhythmic change, augmentation and diminuation are good when new color is desired; also the transposition of a fragment of a motive to a higher or lower octave. These adjustments are made to aid the imitation in its harmonic construction and add new color, but they should not infringe upon the recognition of the original motive.

THE INVENTION

The invention is the least constrained of the three principal classes of polyphonic form and it takes more liberties in its structural design than the other forms. It may be composed in sections and there are three in all. (The number of sections used is optional but three are basic.) The number of measures to a section is optional = 8 – 11 – 6 – 7 – 13, etc.

THE MOTIVE

The motive (theme) is simple, brief and in melodic form. It should be at least a measure in length but not more than two. Its first two or three tones should give a strong tonic impression. The motive serves as the thematic *germ* for the entire composition.

THE EPISODE

To all of those portions of each section in which the motive does not appear, the term *episode* (or episodic passage) is applied. Its main function is to break the monotony of the constant repetition of the motive and to maintain a balance in the tonality. They should be brief, not more than one or two, maybe three measures in length. The material for the episode is taken from the motive or the counterpoint, along with some new material to give it originality. It is not in itself a musical aim but a marriage of material taken from the motive and the counterpoint.

THE SEQUENCE

The sequence brings regularity and symmetry to the thematic development and is an aid for the beginner. With its use the student does not have to search for thematic material. When you are at a loss for ideas use the sequence and it will in itself introduce many ideas; use however, not more than three or four at a time. A larger number is permissible if the motive is very short. The sequence is wonderful for modulating into new keys or even maintaining a tonality simply by moving upward or downward a few intervals.

THE 1ST SECTION

When the 1st section begins in major, the close will be in the key of the dominant, C major to G major (Ex. 21Ⓐ). When the 1st section begins in minor, the close will be in the relative major key, C minor to Eb major (Ex. 21Ⓑ).

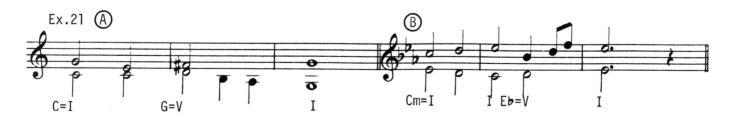

Routine for 1st Section	Motive	C.P. 1 Imit. of Motive	Seq. or Imit. of Motive	An Episode modulating into a closing key.
	Motive C.P. 2	Seq. or Imit.	Seq. or short episode leading into V — I. Imit.	

1st SECTION

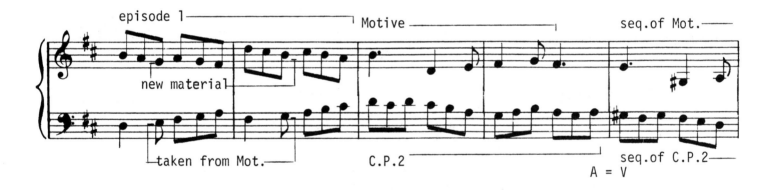

Assignment

Analyze Ex. 22 making sure that you understand thoroughly all of its principals. Review page 15 and *compare* its *text* to the *1st section* of Ex. 22. Then, write a motive or select any simple two measure theme to start with. Don't try anything complex as yet. The idea is to get a working knowledge of its construction.

16

2ND SECTION

The 2nd section starts in the key in which the 1st section ends. This section employs new counterpoints, new figures in the episode and also some related material from the 1st section. The motive is the same, though for variety it may be in contrary motion. The formation is the same as in the 1st section and it ends in any related key—most of the time the sub-dominant. Ex. 23 shows a complete analysis of the 2nd section.

2nd SECTION

Ex.23

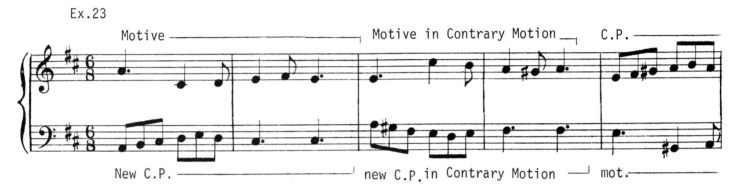

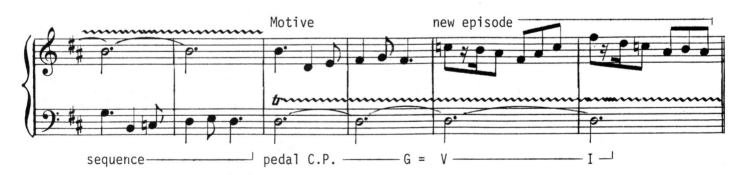

Assignment

Analyze the 2nd section and add a 2nd to your 1st section using Ex. 23 as a model.

3RD SECTION

This section may begin in any key, but most of the time it begins in the sub-dominant of the closing key (the closing key is the key of the composition). The routine is the same as in the 1st and 2nd sections but with still more new ideas for color. Augmentation may be used along with embellishments of the motive, by enlarging its intervals, shifting the rhythm, the use of the non-harmonic elements which disguise the first note of the motive. All of these devices can be put to use in this 3rd and final section. The section ends in the original key with a much more pronounced V to I than that which is used for the 1st and 2nd sections (Ex. 24).

3rd SECTION

Ex.24

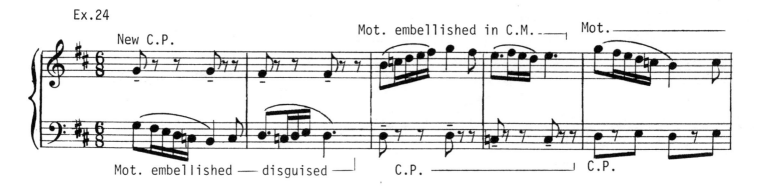

Assignment

Thoroughly analyze this 3rd section and write a 3rd section to your original invention. You are also to copy this 1st invention (Ex. 22, 23 and 24) in your notebook forming a complete musical composition. Play these examples on an instrument to hear what they sound like and write as many more as you can. It is necessary to do many exercises to get the feel of polyphonic writing.

In the Two-Part Invention below look for new counterpoint, new episode; see if the motive is enlarged or reduced. Look for embellishments of the motive—they can easily be disguised (see Ex. 24).

Ex.25

Moderato

TWO-PART INVENTION
(Minor)

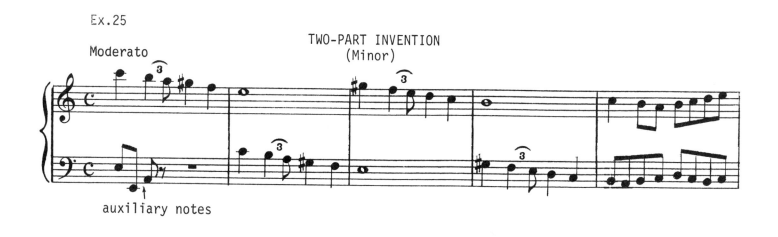

auxiliary notes

C=II   V   I

G = V   I   Dm -V

Dm=I

Codetta

Am=V   I

THREE-PART POLYPHONY

Three-part counterpoint has a more defined chord structure than that of two-part. The parts follow the rules of harmony more strictly and one must use every trick in polyphonic writing to give each part a feeling of originality. The best way to start is by first writing in two parts leaving a place for a third part to be superimposed. Once this third part is superimposed, it will give the composition a harmonic chord structure. It should be disguised by auxiliary tones, neighboring tones and passing tones but in itself it should sound well as an independent melody. The use of the "tie" is necessary. It holds the harmonic fiber together. You must not move all three parts at the same time and by using the "tie," it gives one of the parts a rest while the other two are in motion. Thirds and sixths play a very important part. Two parts move in 3rd and 6th while the third part moves in contrary motion or is sustained by a "tie" or one part is held by a "tie" and the other parts move in contrary motion. When one part has been in motion long enough to state its musical phrase, it may rest, but when a part takes a rest it should be for at least a measure or two. The best places are at the close of a cadence or at any point in the section when it falls upon a tone that has no further obligation, which is some form of tonic harmony. It is best to end a part on an accented beat or a fraction thereof before taking a rest. When the part re-enters it should be on an unaccented beat or a fraction thereof. It is also wise to give a part the motive for its entrance or some other important phrase. As you progress in polyphonic writing, you will find that it is sometimes best to let one part take the lead. You may write this lead part alone, even if it's for 8 measures or more, then fill in the other parts afterwards.

THREE-PART COUNTERPOINT

Ex. 26 Ⓐ: Parallel 4th and 5th are allowed in three (or more) part counterpoint (Ex. 26 Ⓑ). You should strive for complete harmony.

Try writing a two part counterpoint—first with the mental reservation that a 3rd part will be added. Duet writing is necessary but not always between the same pair of voices (Ex. 27).

Ex. 28 Ⓐ: Using measure displacement one creates a sort of free counterpoint. Select the first 8 measures of any song and write a three-part counterpoint using measure displacement.

Ⓑ: All voices in the same quasi rhythm (as in the first species). One voice should move in contrary motion. These examples (Ex. 30 Ⓐ and Ⓑ) are good for small combos like Trumpet, Trombone and Tenor Sax.

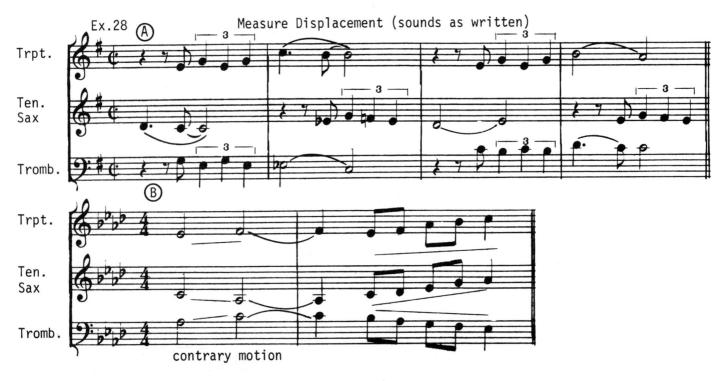

THE THREE-PART CANON

The three-part canon follows the same form as that in two-part (see Page 12), the only difference being that it is written with a third voice. Ex. 29 Ⓐ shows three-part canon with imitation in the octave. Ex. 29 Ⓑ shows three-part canon with imitation in the 5th, but the most practical is the imitation in the octave; it offers less problems in its harmonic structure. The canon is almost *always performed alone.* However, it is possible to add the bass and rhythm to its performance.

FUGATO
(Canon-like)

The fugato is very useful for modulation, introductions and endings. You simply extract a motive from any part of the composition (though the main theme is always the best) and develop it into an intro, ending, etc. Ex. 30 shows an introduction for 2 Trumpets and Trombone with Saxes sustained, using three tonics.

Ex.30

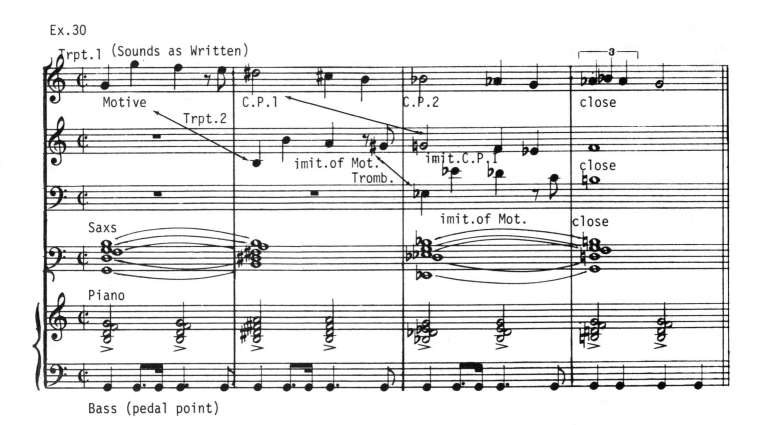

In Ex. 31 Ⓐ Ⓑ are introductions written for two Flutes (1 alto Flute in G) and one Clarinet which were used in a Bossa Nova album that I recorded in France. The motive which is the 1st measure of each example serves as the "germ" for both introductions. Notice how one part will sustain with a "tie" while the others move together or in contrary motion in Ex. 31 Ⓐ and in Ex. 31 Ⓑ. Notice how each part enters right on the motive.

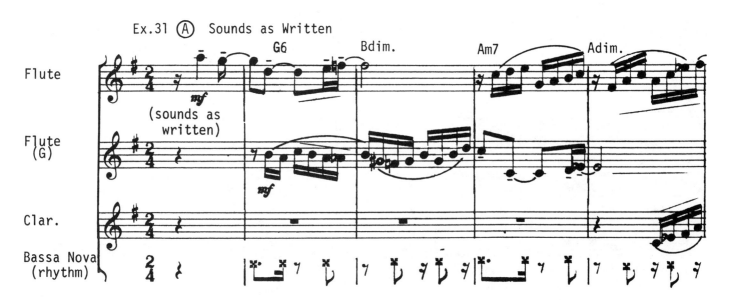

When writing counterpoint for small groups or any type of ensemble, the parts move alone, except perhaps the bass and indefinite pitch instruments such as Drums, Bongos, Conga Drums, Tamborines, etc. Both of these introductions were recorded with a latin rhythm section and nothing more, the other instruments entered at letter A.

Assignment

Write at least 2 examples of all the exercises from Ex. 27 to 31. Select any one or two measure theme and elaborate it into three or four part fugata.

THE STRETTO

   This effect is obtained by starting the imitation before the first statement of the motive has actually finished—creating a kind of contrapuntal imitation. This overlapping of the imitation is like fitting the pieces of a puzzle together. You must keep shifting the imitation backwards note for note until it fits harmonically with the motive. Needless to say, the most practical is the two-part stretto which offers the least problem, but three or four-part stretti is possible. It is best to start the stretto just at about the middle part of the motive (if it is possible), but it can start after the first (2nd or 3rd) note. Just remember that the further back you start the imitation, the more manipulating you will have to do. There are many ways to use the stretto: in contrary motion, by augmentation of diminution, the intervals may be enlarged or reduced; in brief, all of the tricks of polyphonic writing are *available* with the use of the stretto. Ex. 32 Ⓐ shows the original motive; Ⓑ with imitation in the part stretto; Ⓒ with imitation in three part stretto and Ⓓ shows an 8 measure phrase done in stretto for four instruments.

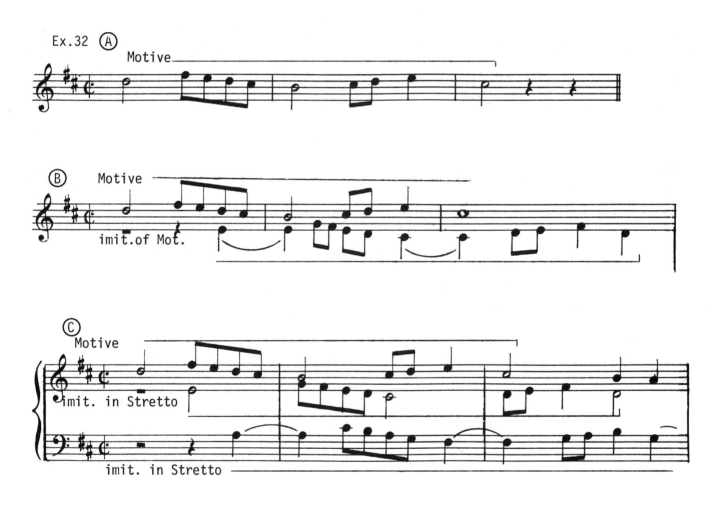

Assignment

Write two-part stretto—first with very simple themes; then try three and four parts.

THE THREE-PART INVENTION

The motive in a three-part invention is not as lively as that of the two-part invention. It is also smaller in compass. Since there are three parts, the motive must cover a smaller range. The motive may start the first statement in any voice, but it is most often the inner voice. The 1st imitation is in the next higher or lower voice and the best imitation is the imitation in the 5th. The 2nd imitation is almost certain to be in the octave of the 1st announcement. However, in many cases the 2nd imitation is not announced until after the first two parts have announced the motive two or three times and then after a brief episode the third announcement is made. If the lower part does not make the first statement of the motive it generally takes up an accompaniment part which establishes the tonality and rhythm of the composition.

As for the remaining sections, they follow the same formula as the two-part invention (which you should review). The stretto is used along with the other devices such as contrary motion, augmentation, diminuation, etc. Ex. 33 shows the 1st section of a three part invention thoroughly.

THREE-PART INVENTION
(1st Section)

Ex.33

Assignment

As you can see, in this first section certain liberties have been taken. Once you understand the formula you can write your inventions as you please. (After all, the name of the composition is "an invention.") This invention in its entirety is analyzed completely in Ex. 34. You are to study it, then analyze Ex. 35, 36, and 37. Look for all of the devices that are used in polyphonic writing because they are all there. Write at least two three-part inventions from original motives; one in major, one in minor.

Ex.34

Andante

Motive ⌐⎯⎯⎯⎯⎯⎯⎯⎤

*A modulation to Bb Major modulating chromatically to Am—a distant key.

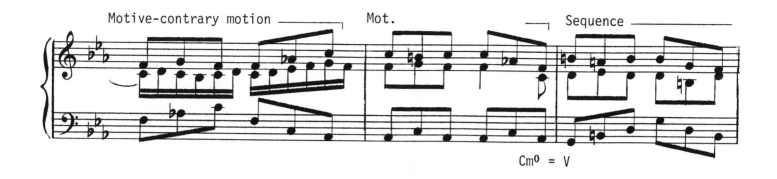

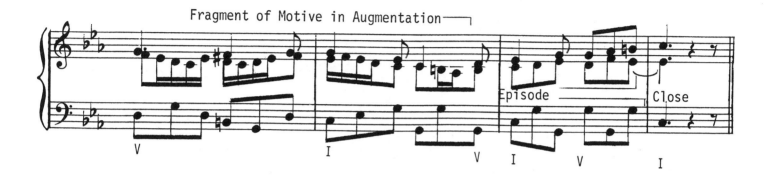

FOUR-PART INVENTION

The four-voice invention follows the same rules as those of the two and three voices and it takes even more liberties. If the first statement is made in an upper voice, its imitation can follow in the next lower or higher voice, but it does not have to follow this rule. The 1st statement when made in the soprano can be imitated in the tenor or bass rather than the alto. It can start alone or with one or all of the other voices together as accompaniment; it can be imitated on any interval and in any voice at random. However, with four voices, the motive should move at a slower pace and its length should not exceed more than one measure. Avoid wide skips in this type of polyphony and use stepwise motion as much as possible. The use of the "tie," rest, parallel 3rd and 6th and sustained rhythm are the secret to the writing of good four-part polyphony.

FOUR-PART INVENTION

32

Am =V   I

V   I

THE FUGUE

The main difference between a fugue and an invention is that the invention only follows the general form of counterpoint whereas the fugue is more strict and follows certain special conditions and limitations which are as follows: the subject (or theme—but the word *theme* applies to all polyphonic music while the word *subject* only means the first statement of a fugue) is more extended, its form is more definite than that of the *motive* and it makes its 1st announcement alone. In the first section it is announced alternately in the tonic and dominant keys. What follows the first statement is known as the *response* which is announced a perfect 5th above or a perfect 4th below the first statement. Before the subject is announced a 2nd time, a brief episode of a measure or two is inserted to add variety and act as a *means of modulation* back to the original key where the subject will make its 2nd announcement an 8*va* higher or lower, which in turn is followed by the 2nd response in the remaining voice. This is again followed by an episode of any length in which still another announcement of the subject may be made. The first section or exposition then ends with a perfect cadence in the dominant key from a major beginning and in the relative major key from a minor beginning. This is only a general rule for a close of the first section because it is possible to close in *any key* relative or remote, even in the principal key itself.

After the close of the first section the fugue follows the same form as that of the invention. There is no special rule as to how often the subject appears or as to what scale step it should appear on for the remaining sections.

When composing the subject for a fugue one must be primarily concerned as to how it is constructed. It is best to start the theme on the 1st or 3rd step in tonic harmony and it is *necessary* that the theme has a decided tonic impression. It must be remembered that the response is a *strict imitation of the subject* in the perfect 5th which means that every interval is an exact imitation of a perfect 5th above or a perfect 4th below the subject. If there is a strong tonic impression there is no problem but if there is a dominant impression, problems begin. Ex. 38 shows a subject with a tonic impression and its response. There are no adjustments necessary, it is a perfect imitation. It starts on the 3rd and ends on the 3rd and offers no problems. Analyze this example.

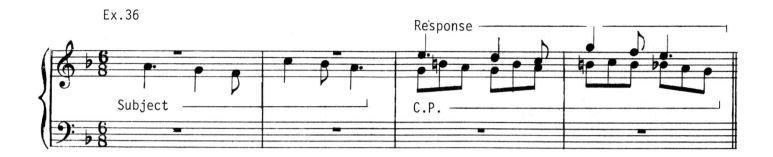

Ex.36

Response

Subject

C.P.

Now Ex. 37 Ⓐ shows an example of a subject with a strong dominant impression with its response in the pefect 5th. If you will play this phrase on the piano, it will probably shock you because it modulates abruptly from the key of E minor to the key of B minor. What causes this is the fact that the 5th is the opening tone in the subject and all of the other notes in the phrase are leaning upon it for support; when it is imitated a perfect 5th higher it becomes the dominant of the dominant, which causes a very abrupt and awkward modulation.

By analyzing this subject we see that all of the tones in it except 4 are actually part of a B7th chord. That is why they are inseparable from the dominant and if you analyze still further you will find that two of the remaining 4 tones could very easily be upper and lower neighbors (Ex. 37 NB).

Ex.37 Ⓐ

Ⓑ B7

N.B.

To eliminate this abrupt modulation in such dominant phrases as these, the imitation is made in the perfect 4th (Ex. 38), causing the leading tone to fall on the note E which retains the original key feeling for an instant and allows a movement to adjust itself to the modulation. This is known as the *tonal response.*

Ex.38

Response

Subject

C.P.

There are many instances where it is necessary to imitate certain tones in the perfect 4th and these tones are most often the 5ths. Ex. 39 shows an example where only the first four tones are imitated in the perfect 4th while the remaining tones are imitated in the perfect 5th. Analyze Ex. 41. If you pay attention to the 5th when it is in the beginning of the subject and imitate it in the perfect 4th, your ear will tell you if it is necessary to imitate the remaining tones in the perfect 4th or the perfect 5th.

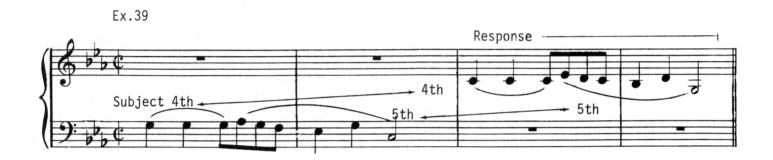

THE EXPOSITION

Exercise 40 Ⓐ: The subject is announced entirely alone in upper voice. Ⓑ: The response is a perfect 4th below in the next lower voice. Ⓒ: An episodic passage (which is taken from the subject) of one measure. Ⓓ: The subject is announced a 2nd time in the next lower voice. Ⓔ: The response in the remaining voice (notice that though the response starts in the lowest voice the 2nd half is taken up by its parallel voice). This can be done at any time but it is best to start this type of polyphony *after the first section*. Ⓕ: Still another episodic passage, this of two measures. Ⓖ: And in the last two measures which modulate first to Eb major then to C minor, there is another subject in the 5th which closes the first section.

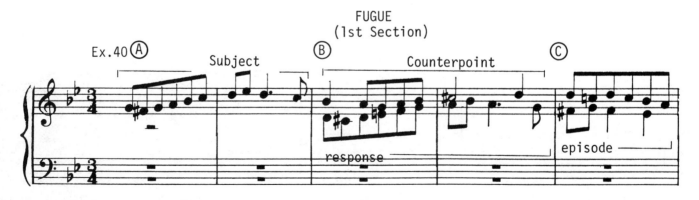

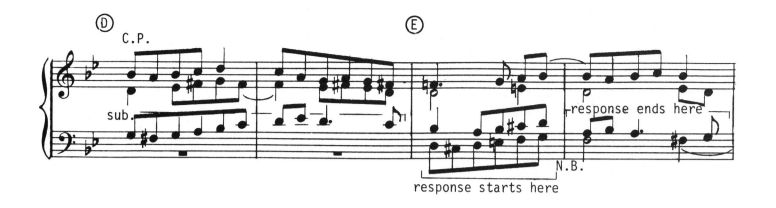

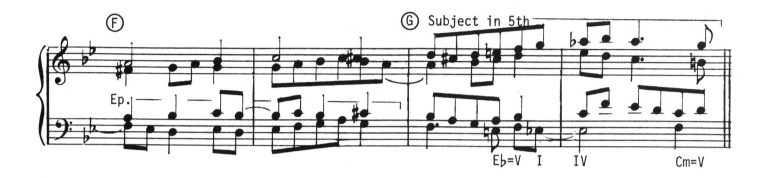

THE REMAINING SECTIONS

As stated on page 34, one has the same liberty in the remaining section as in those of the invention. The themes may overlap as in the stretto, they may be augmented, diminished, imitated by contrary motion, etc.

There are many new ideas in music today that did not exist in the days of Bach, which are wonderful for the development of the remaining section. It is wise for the student to write his fugues on some type of chord structure (this will help tremendously with the leading of the four parts) until he has the feel of polyphonic writing. After the 1st section, by using rhythmic outline, symmetric harmony and chromatic harmony, many problems can be solved. Ex. 41Ⓐ shows a chromatic chord cycle. Ⓑ: The rhythmic outline of Fugue No. 1 (Ex. 40). Ⓒ: The subject reproduced, but in rhythm only. This is actually the opening measure to the 2nd section of Fugue No. 1 (page 38).

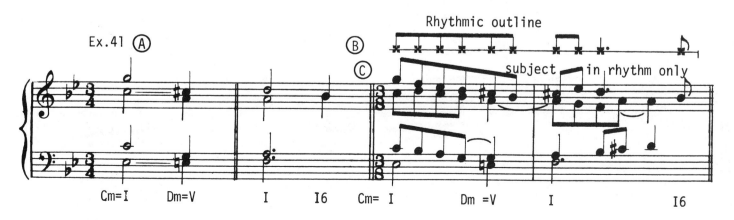

FUGUE

1st half of subject

2nd half of subject

38

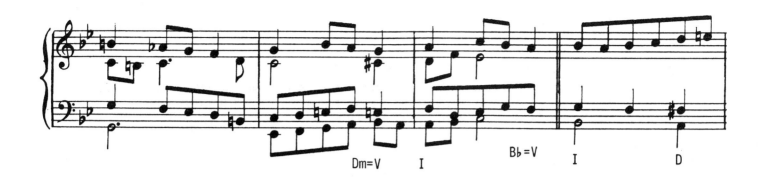

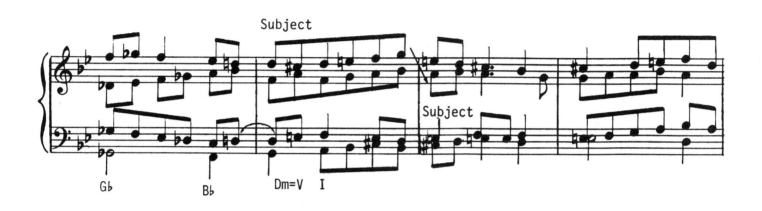

The *two-voice fugue* is somewhat limited in scope. However, its subject can be lively and takes in a wider range than the other forms; the episodic passages have much more freedom and more brilliance as a rule.

The *three-voice fugue* is also a lively composition but it follows just about the same formula as that of four voices: subject, response, a brief episodic passage then subject an 8*va* lower or higher; it is optional to have another response, but if there is one, it is an 8*va* higher or lower than the 1st response. What follows this is a long episode which modulates into the new key (also optional).

The *five-voice fugue* is soprano, alto, tenor, bass and the fifth voice is either 2nd soprano, tenor or bass, rarely 2nd alto. The announcements are subject, response, episodic passage, subject, response, subject. Here again it is necessary to stress the importance of the "tie," the sustained tones, the rest and the use of many 3rds and 6ths. In the five-voice fugues, the theme is not so active and the entire texture has more or less a chord form. When it is possible to sustain a tone do so, when it is possible to let a tone rest, do so.

CONCLUSION

Review two-part counterpoint; notice how the counterpoint always follows the theme. When the theme is in contrary motion, so is the counterpoint. This device is a good one to use at all times because if a counterpoint is good, it can reappear from time to time in a different section or in an episodic passage. This gives form to your composition. When the counterpoint follows the theme in every announcement of the *1st section*, it is known as a double counterpoint. Make a few sketches of a theme with a good counterpoint, put the counterpoint above, below and then write them both in contrary motion with the counterpoint above and below.

Part II

ORCHESTRATION

The art of arranging (orchestrating) cannot be taught by rules, but its technique can and must be learned. This technique must be acquired in one way or another before good arranging becomes possible. The best system of acquiring this knowledge is through the analysis of the works written in the past and those by contemporary composers.

It is not eough that the arranger be acquainted with only one or two different styles of orchestration. He must have a working knowledge of all accepted styles. This equipment must be diversified and ample in scope. Of course, the symphonic type must be well established; then there is the grand contrapuntal style of the past centuries; the resulting expressionistic treatments of the nineteenth century; the Romantic development; the Impressionistic designs; the atonal and polyphonic evolutions of our time; the current progressive jazz, free jazz, rock 'n roll, etc.

The art of arranging music for the orchestra requires an understanding of the compass (range), tone quality and the technical possibilities of the orchestral instruments.

The material presented in this book deals exclusively with the problems of orchestration and so the knowledge of harmony, and counterpoint is a prerequisite.

The radio, TV, concerts and fine recordings so readily available, it would be regrettable were the student not to grasp the opportunities afforded by them; from them he can gain a working knowledge of orchestral treatment.

The instruments used in the symphony orchestra are in the following order: Strings — Woodwind — Brass — Percussion. These departments are discussed in full detail in the following pages.

INSTRUMENTATION

THE VIOLIN

Ex. 1 (A): The violin employs the G clef, exclusively. (B): Strings which are played and not touched by the fingers are called open strings. (C): The complete range of the violin. (D): The most practical range.

The term *sul* means that all of the written notes are to be played upon the same string. Ex. 2: The highest *sul* for the G, D and A strings is about a major 9th; but the E string is played to its limit.

NATURAL HARMONICS

Natural harmonics are obtained by lightly touching the notes on the strings thus breaking up into subsidiary vibrations. On the violin each string has five natural harmonics.

By lightly touching the E string (half-way between the nut and bridge) one produces the tone E one octave higher (Ex. (A)); touching the string 1/3 of its length from the nut (which is a perfect fifth) the tone B one octave higher is produced (Ex. (B)); lightly touching the string 1/4 of its length from the nut (a perfect fourth) the resulting tone produced is an E two octaves higher (Ex. (C)); going on to the string 1/5 of its length from the nut (a major third) G# one octave higher is produced (Ex. (D)); finally, by lightly touching the string 1/6 of its length from the nut (a minor third) the tone B two octaves higher is produced (Ex. (E)).

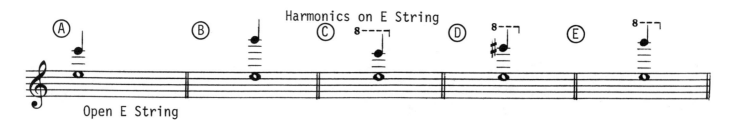

Harmonics on E String

Open E String

Natural Harmonics are produced in the same manner on the remaining stringed instruments (Ex. Ⓕ).

Open A String   Open D String   Open G String

In practice, harmonic No. 5 is not used because it can be produced more easily and with better tone quality as harmonic No. 3 on the next higher string.

To indicate the notation for natural harmonic, one simply places an "o" over each tone that is to be played as a harmonic. It should also be indicated in the music on which string the harmonics are to be taken. The Italian word *sul I, sul II, sul III,* etc. (on first, second or third string) is used for this indication (Ex. Ⓖ).

Sul II ——————————— Sul III ——————— Sul II ———————

ARTIFICIAL HARMONICS

Artificial harmonics are obtained by lightly touching the strings with the fourth finger while sustaining a given tone with the first finger, a perfect fourth below. If the student will look at harmonic No. 3 in the natural harmonic series, he will notice that with use of the open string one simply touches the string a perfect fourth higher to produce the open tone two octaves higher as a harmonic. Ex. Ⓐ shows the natural harmonic which produces the tone D, two octaves higher (harmonic No. 3). Ex. Ⓑ shows the same tone produced with the *artifical harmonic* on the G string. This is achieved by placing the first finger at the fourth position on the G string and lightly touching the string with the fourth finger.

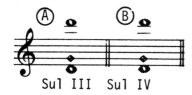

Sul III   Sul IV

When writing artificial harmonics, it's not necessary to write out three different notes as in the above examples. One simply writes the desired tone or tones two octaves lower than the required sound. Then by placing a small diamond ◆ a fourth above each note the musician will know that they are to be played as *artificial harmonics,* sounding two octaves higher (Ex. Ⓒ).

Sul III _____

The compass of useful natural harmonics are shown in Ex. Ⓓ.

By adding the Artificial Harmonic to the Natural,
we get the following complete compass:

THE VIOLA

Ex. 3Ⓐ: The viola is written mostly in the alto clef (C clef). Ⓑ: A good working *device* when writing for this instrument is to place each tone a *letter lower* than concert, plus an octave higher. Ⓒ: *Not a tone lower* but *a letter lower.* The accidentals, if any, will be carried along.

Ex. 4Ⓐ: The open strings for the viola as written. Ⓑ: The open strings as they sound. The G (treble) clef is used for the extreme high tones, however, the point of change from alto to treble clef is not fixed. Ⓒ: The complete range. Ⓓ: Most useful range. Ⓔ: The highest *sul* for the viola (as for the violin) is about a major 9th for the C, G and D strings. Ⓕ: The A string is played to its limit.

NATURAL HARMONICS

The technique and notation of natural harmonics are the same for the Viola as those of the Violin; however, they are to be transposed down a perfect fifth.

ARTIFICIAL HARMONICS

Here again technique and notation is the same as for the Violin. Ex. Ⓐ shows a complete compass of the harmonics, both natural and artificial. This example is diagrammed similar to that for the Violin.

THE CELLO

Ex. 5Ⓐ: The cello is written mostly in the bass clef (F clef). Ⓑ: But for the extreme high notes the G (treble) clef is used. Ⓒ: The tenor clef *is used* also. In order to read scores, it is necessary to have a knowledge of the tenor clef. The tenor clef is written a letter plus an octave higher than concert and the accidentals if any are carried along.

THE OPEN STRINGS FOR THE CELLO
Ex. 6 Ⓐ

Ex. 6 Ⓑ: The complete compass. Ⓒ: Most useful range. The *sul* (as with the violin and viola) is about a major 9th for the C, G and D string while the A string is playable to its full limit.

NATURAL HARMONIC

Again, the technique and notation for the Cello are the same as that for the Violin and Viola. The only adjustment to be made is transposing that of one Violin down a twelfth.

ARTIFICIAL HARMONIC

Although the technique is the same and transposed down a twelfth, the Cello has a more extended limit than the Violin and Viola. Ex. Ⓐ shows the complete compass of both the natural and artificial harmonics. This example is diagrammed similar to that of the Violin.

THE DOUBLE BASS

Ex. 7 Ⓐ: The double bass is written in the bass clef. Ⓑ: Its complete compass. Ⓒ: Its most useful range; it sounds an octave lower.

NATURAL HARMONICS

Harmonics of the Bass are best produced on the first and second strings where all five natural harmonics are available. Although harmonics are available on the third and fourth strings, some of them are little more than scratches as far as tonal quality goes. Since the Bass is a transposing instrument (sounds an octave lower than written) it is best to write the harmonics at the actual pitch, adding the direction "actual pitch" and with the usual harmonic sign "o" above each note.

In practice the most useful harmonics may be reduced to those of Ex. Ⓐ.

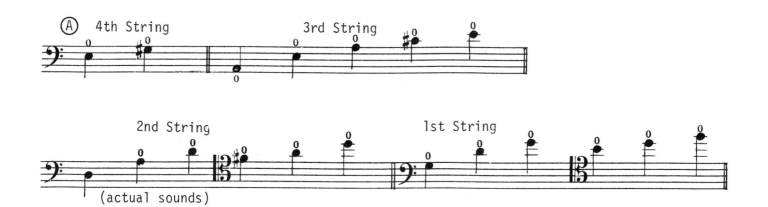

(actual sounds)

ARTIFICIAL HARMONICS

These are not practical for orchestral use. Only the finest Bass soloist is capable of achieving clarity. Therefore, in this study they are not included.

THE FLUTE IN C

Ex. 8Ⓐ: Complete compass.   Ⓑ: Most useful range.   Ⓒ: Low register requires transparent background.   Ⓓ: Middle register is strong but still needs light background.   Ⓔ: High register is strong, clear and brilliant.   Ⓕ: two trills are impossible.   Ⓖ: All other trills are possible but no trills above high G.

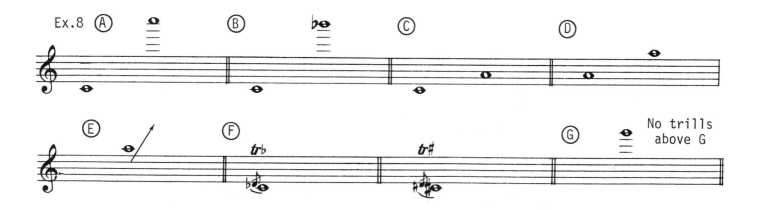

THE FLUTE IN G (ALTO)

The alto flute in G is written a perfect 4th above concert (Ex. 9Ⓐ). The high register of this flute is not needed but the low register has a better quality than the regular C flute.

THE PICCOLO IN C

This is a small flute. The written range is from D below the staff to Bb (*8va*) above the staff. This sounds an octave higher than written. The upper register is shrill and piercing and needs the support of a large orchestra. The lower octave is too weak for average use, although effective when the background is light. It is seldom used as solo, but to double other wood wind solos at the octave or double octave. The 2nd flutist (or in a large orchestra, the 3rd flutist) doubles on the piccolo (Ex. 10 Ⓐ and Ⓑ).

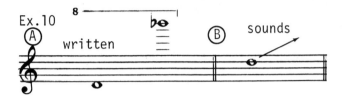

THE OBOE (IN C)

A double reed instrument with a penetrating, nasal tone (Ex. 11Ⓐ). The range is from Bb below the staff to G (four lines above). Ⓑ: From high C up-wards the tone becomes thin, and unpleasant, the flute is more desirable in that register. Ⓒ: The oboe is essentially a melodic instrument, and it is difficult to assign it to filling out tones in the sustaining harmony as it can easily become too prominent. The best range for such an effect (Ex. 11Ⓒ) is E to E in the staff. Ⓓ: The best range for solos is from D below the staff to Bb a line above.

The staccato may be very rapid and notes may be repeated fairly rapidly. The lower tones are rich when at a dynamic of *mf* or more. This register should be used economically as too much of it will become monotonous (Ex. 12Ⓐ). Trills should not be written from D above the staff upwards. All others are very agile. The oboe requires plenty of wind, so take it easy on the player and give him enough breathing spells.

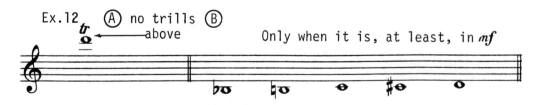

THE ENGLISH HORN (Cor Anglais) IN F

A large oboe. The written compass is from B below the staff to D above. This sounds a perfect 5th lower. Chiefly used for solo work, where an expressive tone quality is needed. The best and most characteristic register of the instrument is at the lower octave and a half. It may be used as an inner voice in the wood wind ensemble but tends to be prominent as with the oboe. It doubles well with violas, cellos and with low clarinets (Ex. 13 Ⓐ, Ⓑ).

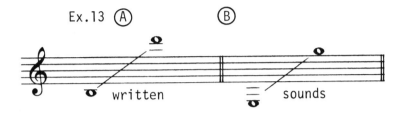

THE CLARINET (Bb and A)

Two clarinets are in use, the Bb and the A. The Bb is the most common. The Bb clarinet is written a whole tone up, and the A clarinet a minor third up (above concert). The written range is from E below the staff to C (8va) above. This sounds a tone lower, on the Bb clarinet and a minor third lower on the A clarinet (Ex. 14 Ⓐ, Ⓑ, Ⓒ).

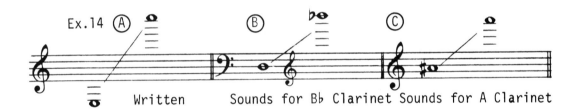

The bottom register is extremely characteristic, being rich and sinister. The top note in this register is Bb in the staff (written for the instrument). For solo work, the written tone E should be the limit, for the average player. Of course, some soloists can perform pleasingly at a much higher range, but the top notes are apt to be too squeaky and shrill for anything except exaggerated effects (Ex. 15 Ⓐ, Ⓑ, Ⓒ).

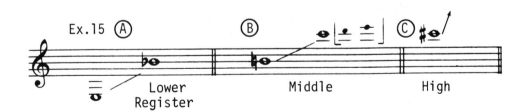

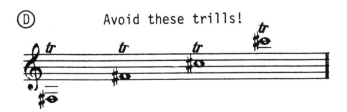

THE Eb CLARINET

This instrument, which has always been in use in military bands, was introduced to the concert orchestra at the beginning of the 20th century. Berlioz was probably the first to make use of it in the orchestra and such composers as Schoenberg, Varese and Berg have employed its sound in their music.

The Eb Clarinet is written a minor third lower than it sounds. Ex. Ⓐ shows the written compass while Ex. Ⓑ shows the actual sound.

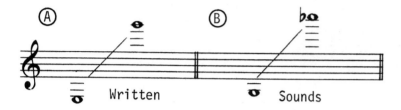

The sounds of this instrument has a hard biting quality and its upper register is the most useful. The lower half should not be used in ensemble and rarely in solo work. The most useful compass is shown in Ex. Ⓒ.

The Eb Clarinet is more practical in the upper octave than the Flute, which lacks character in the forte passages or the Oboe which is useless in the upper register. Ex. Ⓓ shows voicings with the Eb Clarinet on top. Ex. Ⓔ shows a staccato passage in concerted harmony with two Bb Clarinets.

The Eb Clarinet is a most agile instrument; any manner of leaps and jumps are possible. Ex. Ⓕ is a good example.

THE BASS CLARINET (Bb)

This is a large clarinet, which sounds an octave below the small clarinet. The part is written in the treble clef a major 9th higher than the concert notes. Most bass clarinets have the low Eb. There is no A bass clarinet. The bass clarinet forms a strong bass for the woodwind group often voiced below the bassoons. The lower octave is full and rich. It is often used as a solo instrument. When doubled with cello, bass, etc., it provides strong definition and clarity to the bass line. The upper register is *not useful when played alone* but good when doubling other instruments in a middle register (Ex. 16 Ⓐ, Ⓑ).

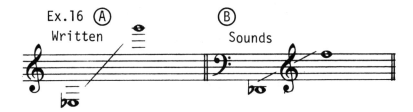

Ex. 16 Ⓐ Written   Ⓑ Sounds

THE BASSOON

This is a double reed instrument. The range is from Bb below the bass staff to Bb, 3rd line of the treble staff. Higher tones can be produced but the Bb is the safest high note. The part is written in the bass clef for the low register and in the tenor clef for the extreme high tones (Ex. 17).

The main function of the bassoon is to supply the bass for the woodwind choir. But, it is also useful for melody either as a solo or when doubled by another member of the woodwinds in octaves or in unison. Bassoons and clarinets are a good blend; and two bassoons and two French horns are a good alternative for four horns.

It is very agile, with a very strong staccato. The low register is strong and very rich in texture. The middle and upper registers are adapted to melodic lines that require an expressive quality.

Ex. 17

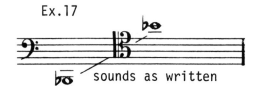

sounds as written

CONTRA-BASSOON

This is comparable to the string bass and like it sounds an octave lower than written. Its main function is to strengthen the bass line. It is not flexible and should have a simple part with plenty of rests. The best use is for ensemble. The high tones are of little value (Ex. 18).

Ex. 18
Sounds 8th lower_____

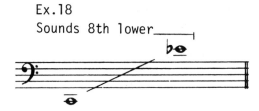

THE HORN IN F (French Horn)

This horn had no valves until about one hundred years ago. Therefore, "crooks" were needed to place the horn in the desired key. This accounts for the many different notations such as, horn in C, horn in D, horn in E, etc. When valves were added to the horn, it became a chromatic instrument and so the "crooks" were no longer necessary. Because of this, the horn in F is the only horn that need be considered in today's orchestrations. The bass clef is used for the lowest register and the treble clef for the upper register. The part for horn in F is written a perfect 5th *above* concert, whether in *bass or treble clef*. (In older music the parts in bass clef were transposed a perfect 4th *below* the concert notes, but the adjustment is no longer legitimate.) The actual sound of the horn in F therefore is a perfect 5th below the written notes (Ex. 19 Ⓐ, Ⓑ). The tones at the highest and lowest range of the horn are difficult to produce so the best range is from C in the bass clef to G above the treble staff (Ex. 19 Ⓒ, Ⓓ).

The horn is often used for expressive passages in the register from C below the staff to E in the staff (Ex. 19 Ⓔ, Ⓕ).

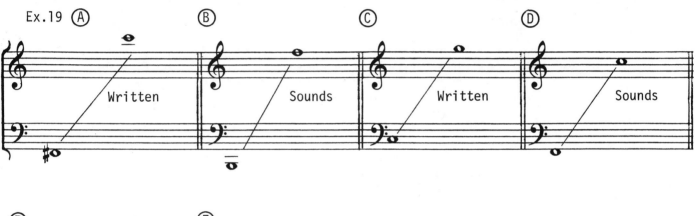

The horn may be used for strong attacks, especially when the bell is stopped by the hand. Such stopped notes are marked with a + over each note.

For echo effects, a mute can be inserted into the bell of the horn (after a few measures of rest). This is marked "con sordino."

Moving parts in the low register are not advised. Write sustained tones in this area. Although sustaining tones are written a great deal for the horn, repeated tones in groups of two or three are a characteristic effect. Passages that require rapid execution should be doubled by other instruments so as to make the sound more definite. Trills for the horn while possible are better avoided.

Owing to the conical mouthpiece, the player must use different embouchures for the high and low notes. The result of this is the classification of high horn and low horn. Dove-tailing the horns will show that the odd numbers are the high horns and the even numbers the low horns. The limit for high horn is about middle C; the highest for low horn about D in the treble staff (Ex. 20 Ⓐ, Ⓑ). However, this is not a hard and fast rule especially in unison passages for horns.

It is recommended that key-signatures be written for horns in F. The older parts were written without signatures, but this is no longer necessary.

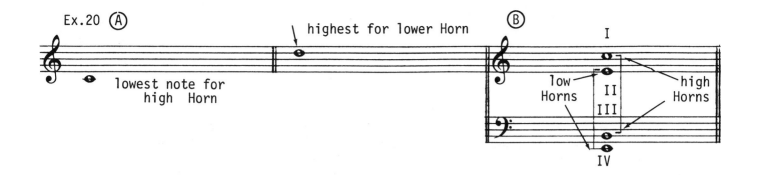

THE BRASS (The Bb Trumpet)

The Trumpet in Bb is the most used in today's music. Ex. 21Ⓐ: Complete compass. Ⓑ: Most useful range. Ⓒ: Double and triple tongueing is not difficult —but not for too long a period of time.

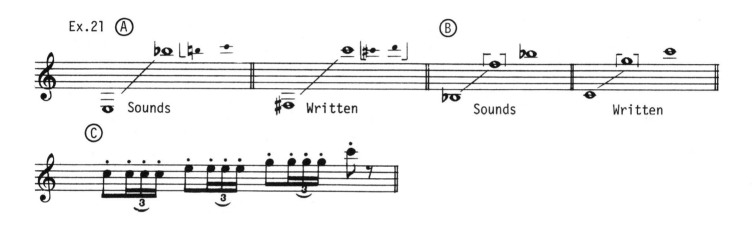

THE TROMBONE (Bb)

This instrument is in Bb but there is no transposition. It is written in bass clef and sounds as written. Ex. 22Ⓐ: Complete compass. Ⓑ: Most useful range. Ⓒ: There are three pedal tones which are possible.

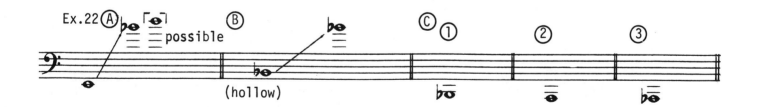

THE BASS TROMBONE

Ex. 23Ⓐ: The bass trombone in G is written in bass clef and sounds as written. There are no pedal tones (Ex. 23Ⓑ). The three trombones sound well as a unit. (See Chart next page.)

THE TUBA

The Tuba is used mainly to double the third trombone, an octave lower (Ex. 23Ⓒ,Ⓓ).

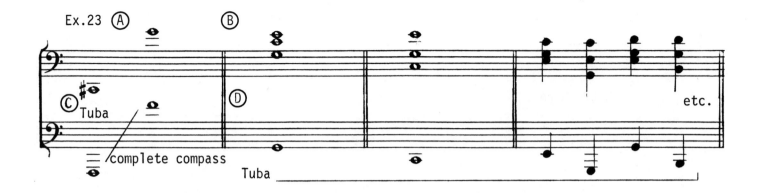

Ex. 24(A) is a chart of the 7 positions on the Bb trombone. When writing for the trombone avoid wide skips into and out of the 7th position and especially into the 1st position (Ex. 24 (B)).

THE HARP

The harp is tuned to the diatonic scale of Cb major. There are seven strings in each register to each of which is attached a pedal — Cb, Db, Eb, Fb, Gb, Ab, Bb. These pedals can be raised one or two notches. When any one of these pedals is depressed one notch, the "letter" is raised one half tone in *all* registers. When depressed two notches, the "letter" is raised a whole tone.

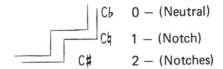

Cb	0 — (Neutral)
C♮	1 — (Notch)
C#	2 — (Notches)

Ex. 25 Ⓐ: Complete compass. In writing glissandi, *every* string must be accounted for. Ex. 25 Ⓑ shows a B7 glissando, which means that Db and Fb are raised two notches and Ab and Bb are raised one notch each creating a B7 chord.

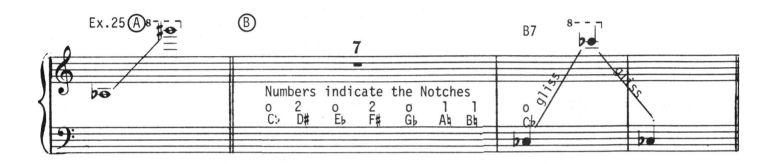

The harpist will tune up to the key signature—then it is only necessary to adjust the tones that are not in the chord (Ex. 26 Ⓐ). Tuning for the key of Db major. Ⓑ: Tuning for a Db 6 chord, then a Db minor 6th chord.

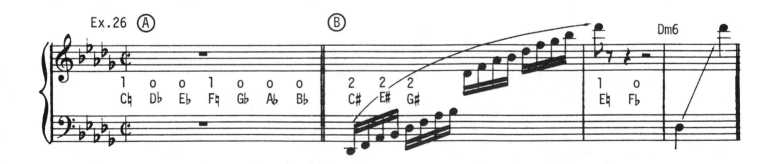

Extreme sharped keys are written in their enharmonic flatted keys = B♮ = Cb, F# = Gb and C# = Db, etc. . . . Ex. 27. Harmonics are produced by lightly touching the middle of the string and sounds an octave higher. The parts often look strange. Ex. 28Ⓐ shows a part written for piano. Ⓑ shows the same part written for the harp.

Ex.27   Harmonic   Sounds

Ex.28 Ⓐ Piano

Ⓑ Harp

PERCUSSION INSTRUMENTS WITH DEFINITE PITCH

THE KETTLE DRUM

Sound is produced by striking the instrument with a soft-headed mallet. The modern compass is produced on three drums. Ex. 29 Ⓐ: The small drum. Ⓑ: The middle. Ⓒ: The large. Today there are in use chromatic kettle drums that change tone almost instantly.

Ex.29 Ⓐ   Ⓑ   Ⓒ

When writing rolls, the accurate length of the roll is written the same as for the bass drum. A chord of two notes can be taken by one man but is not of practical value, except perfect fifths, special effects, or diminished fifths. The kettle drums should be tuned to main harmonic notes of the passage in which they are taking part, which may or may not be *tonic* and *dominant.* Kettle drums are no good if the music is so chromatic as to defy every attempt to bring them into its harmonic scheme.

TWO IMPORTANT POINTS

1. Give the percussionist 2 or 3 bars at least of 4/4 moderate time to make accurate change of a whole tone, and a little longer time for larger intervals.

2. Arrange your part so that the percussionist's new tunings are as small as possible.

Mark clearly in score any altered tunings. (Ex.—Change F to E, C to C# G to A.)

Treat the kettle drums with harmonic value. When writing a crescendo or diminuendo, always state the level you want it to come to and what level to go (Ex. 29 Ⓓ, Ⓔ).

CHIMES

Chimes (tubular) give an imitation of bells and church towers, etc. Ex. 30 Ⓐ: Written and sounds — Bells (plate) used for special effect in orchestra. Ex. 30 Ⓑ: Its written range. Ⓒ: Its sound.

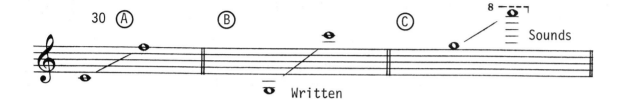

THE XYLOPHONE

The xylophone is capable of producing rapid scales, arpeggios, glissandos, tremolos, double stops, etc. The vibraphone and marimba are only modifications of the xylophone. It sounds as it is written (Ex. 31).

KEY BOARD PERCUSSION
(Instruments)

THE PIANO: Ex. 32Ⓐ: Complete compass. Ⓑ: Most useful range for accompaniment in writing for dance band, popular music, jazz, etc.

The CELESTA. Ex. 32 Ⓒ. The complete compass is used.

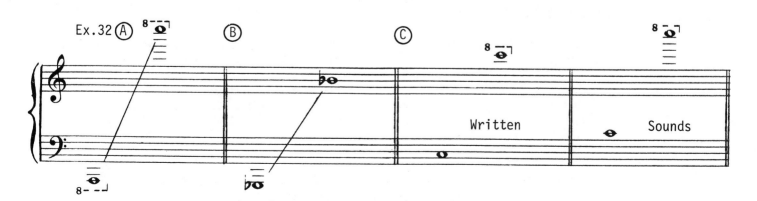

SIDE-DRUM

Ex.33 Notation of Roll

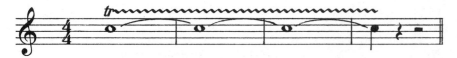

For a strong accent on any beat, omit the slur and mark it ⟩ . This applies to all in the drum family.

Flam: two notes in this rhythm
Open Flam: first note on accented beat
Drag: series of 2, 3, 4, 5 or 6 strokes fused into a sort of instant roll, preceding accented note.

In writing side-drum parts:

1. The tendency is to write too few notes.
2. Never write detached notes.
3. *Drag* and *flam* are only technical ways of accenting effectively a single beat.
4. Any rhythmic combinations can be written.
5. *Long roll* is equally effective p or f but crescendo cannot be spread out long like kettle drums.
6. Always write out in full notes to be played (Ex. 34).

Ex.34

Bass drum muffled

BASS DRUM

Quick rhythmical figures are out of place. *Roll* is practicable and effective. For a specially short note *f* add the word — *muffled.* Two main uses are: 1) To mark highlights, or the progress and climax of a crescendo; 2) To convey feeling of awe and solemnity by means of its pp notes.

TRIANGLE

When a succession of rapid notes are grouped together on a beat (Ex. 35). It is better to use an odd number of strokes.

Tremelo or roll is made by beating rapidly to and fro between two sides of the triangle. At the climax of a crescendo, added triangle is effective. The pp, when used with soft strings and light wood-wind is very good. Single soft strokes mixed with octave unison of a Flute, Oboe and Harp in harmonics sound well. Keep the markings of the triangle below the level of the instruments with which it is playing.

CYMBALS

Tone is produced four ways: 1) Clashing them together (sideways or brushing movements); 2) Striking a single plate with hard side drum stick or soft kettle drum mallot; 3) Agitating the edges of the plates against each other (it must be marked *two plate roll,* it can be used pianissimo to fortissimo); 4) Hanging up single plate and making a roll on it with two soft kettle drum sticks. It is called *two stick roll.* It should be written and the words, *soft drum sticks or timpani sticks,* added above the part. (No. 1 is only effective when used fortissimo at moments of wild excitement. No. 2 in p has a deep gong-like effect. It can be used *p* or *f*. For either of the effects, marke the part *with hard stick or with soft stick.*) Anything from *pp* to *fff* is used. In a two plate roll, two plate stroke, or drum stick roll, mark length of sound required. If minimum, write *minimum.*

GONG

Mostly used for single *p* or *mf* stroke. Cymbals persistent vibration and writing notes of accurate length also apply to the Gong.

TAMBORINE

For detached notes, strike head with knuckles; for roll, shake hoop; for tremolo, rub thumb on head. A sudden unexpected *ff* roll is effective at moments of rhythmic excitement. The *pp* is generally less useful (Ex. 36).

Ex. 36 With thumb

Part III

VOICING

The best voicing, i.e., the best distribution of the tones of a chord, should be made to follow the regular order of the natural harmonic series. In this case, the wide spaces appear at the bottom with the intervals becoming smaller and closer together as the upper register is reached. The inner parts, as demonstrated by the immortal writers, seldom contain open spaces but the two uppermost parts may lie as much as an octave apart. The tones of the natural harmonic series are shown in Ex. 1.

The correct manner of voicing is shown in Ex. 2Ⓐ and follows the distribution of the harmonic series.

The incorrect way of voicing is shown in Ex. 2Ⓑ and it is noticeable that the normal spacing of the harmonic series has been distorted. This applies to all classes of instruments.

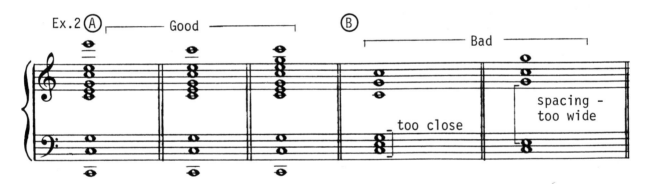

The middle area of the orchestra should be filled in to prevent thinness. To the student of choral writing, this will immediately suggest the tenor upper range as a general region. In Ex. 3Ⓐ the piano voicing is adequate and will sound well at the keyboard. The noticeable wide space between the two hands is of no concern as the vibration (sympathetic) of the piano strings will prevent thinness. In Ⓑ however, when written for orchestra, the inner voices must *actually* be written because there is no other way in which to insure a good sonority.

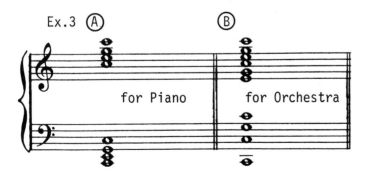

Ex. 4 (A) shows a very satisfactorily voiced part for *piano*. However, if written for orchestra, it would not be good.

The proper way to supply the same chord to the orchestra is as in Ex. 4 (B). Notice that the inner spaces have been correctly filled in.

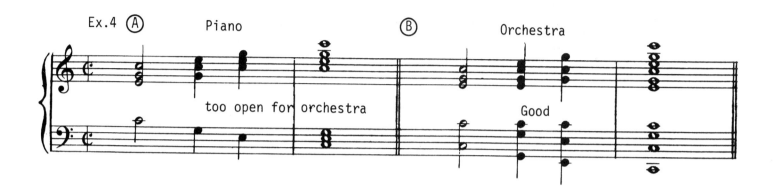

PART WRITING

In the classic technique parallel movement of chords was exceptional; many of the immortal writers had occasion to use the effect with excellent results, e.g., "Les Preludes" (Liszt) employs diminished 7th chords in parallel motion; in "Siegfried" (Wagner) are found augmented triads in parallel motion; Debussy used parallel 7th and 9th chords in root position; Cyril Scott and Arnold Schoenberg and many other master writers used the device to produce very good music. This type of writing will result in 4ths, 5ths and octaves but need not cause concern if properly used. Parallel 5ths are poor only when in two parts; the presence of even *one* more voice will make the effect acceptable (Ex. 5 (A) and (B)).

Parallel octaves (or unisons) are poor when they are used aimlessly and are moving haphazardly (from octaves to harmony, back to octaves, etc.) in parallel motion. However, a melodic line or counterpoint may be duplicated at the octave (or unison) at any time. Also, the bass line may be duplicated at the lower octave and will then provide more depth and resonance. In these cases, the intentional and persistent duplication makes the effect obvious and good.

This newer treatment is not to be understood as dismissing the conventional designs but is submitted only by way of providing greater freedom in writing especially for the different sections of the orchestra.

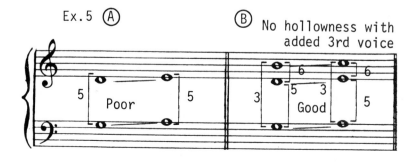

DUET WRITING

Duets should be composed of mostly 3rds and 6ths (Ex. 6).

Ex.6

5ths and 4ths should not be used in succession but should be followed by 3rds and 6ths (Ex. 7 Ⓐ and Ⓑ).

Ex.7 Ⓐ

Ⓑ

TRIO WRITING

With triads, the treatment is obvious, but with 4-part chords, one tone must be omitted. In dealing with chords of the added 6th, there are several possibilities; the 5th may be omitted, the added 6th may be omitted; finally the root may be omitted (Ex. 8 Ⓐ).

With chords of the 7th, omit the root, or omit the 5th, the pure triad may even be used knowing that the chord-7th will be heard (from another direction in the orchestra) (Ex. 8 Ⓑ).

Ex.8 Ⓐ   Ⓑ

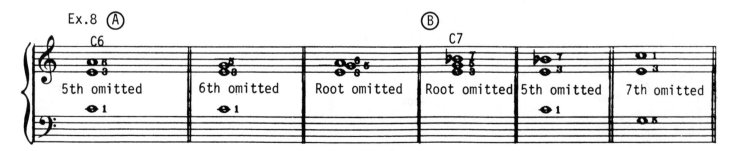

On chords of the 9th, omit the 5th or the root, also you may omit the root and the 5th using the 3, 7, 9 (Ex. 9 Ⓐ).

On 11th chords, use the 7, 9, 11 (Ex. 9 Ⓑ).

On 13th chords, use the 3, 7, 13; also the 1, 3, 13 (Ex. 9 Ⓒ).

4-PART WRITING

With chords that have four different tones such as chords of the added 6th and chords of the 7th, the treatment is obvious.

With chords of the 9th, omit the 5th or omit the root (Ex. 10 Ⓐ).

With 11th chords omit the root (Ex. 10 Ⓑ).

With 13th chords omit the root and 5th using 3, 7, 9, 13; or root and 3rd, using 5, 7, 9, 13; or use 1, 3, 5, 13 (Ex. 10 Ⓒ).

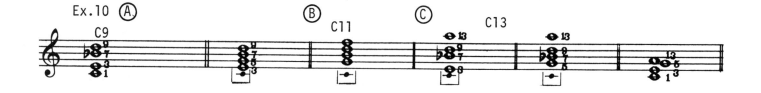

DOUBLE STOPS ON THE VIOLIN, VIOLA AND CELLO

It must be definitely established that no note lower than D (Ex. 11 Ⓐ) can be used as the upper note of a double stop between the D and G strings because the result would be that of the same string G accommodating two tones which is an evident impossibility. By the same token, no tone lower than G (Ex. 11 Ⓑ) can be used as the upper note of a double stop between the G and C strings of the *viola*. As with the viola, no tone lower than G (Ex. 11 Ⓒ) can be used as the upper note of a double stop between the G and the C of the *cello*.

2nds are best avoided unless an open string is used (Ex. 13).

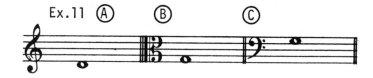

Ex. 12 shows all the 3rds, 4ths, 5ths, 6ths, 7ths and octaves that are practical on the violin as double stops, both major and minor.

Ex.12

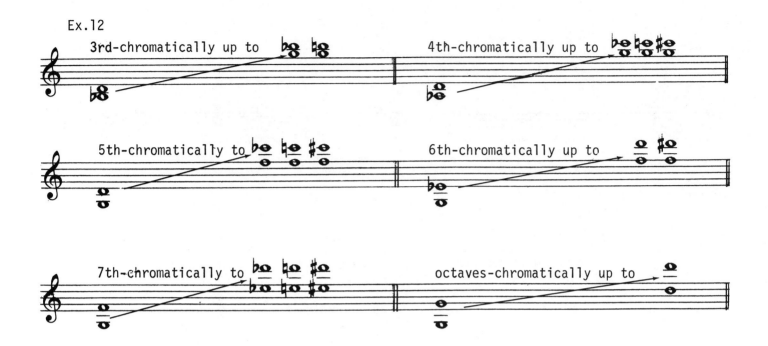

2nds are best avoided unless an open string is used (Ex. 13).

Ex.13

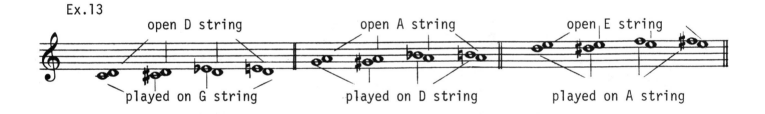

THREE AND FOUR NOTE CHORDS

Try to have at least one open string and add to this a 5th or 6th chord which are easy to play (Ex. 14 Ⓐ). Triple stops (Ex. 14 Ⓑ). Quadruple stops (Ex. 14 Ⓒ). Owing to the curvature of the bridge only the two top notes of three and four note chords can be sustained (Ex. 15). Three and four note chords are best used in *f* or *ff* passages; or when marked or detached chords are in succession.

The foregone double, triple and quadruple stops are available for viola when transposed a perfect 5th lower (Ex. 16 Ⓐ) and for the cello a perfect 5th plus an octave lower (Ex. 16 Ⓑ).

Ex.14 Ⓐ

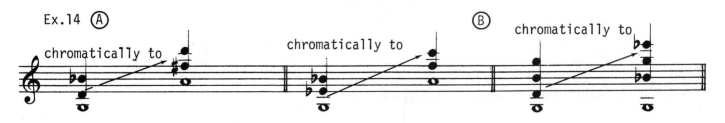

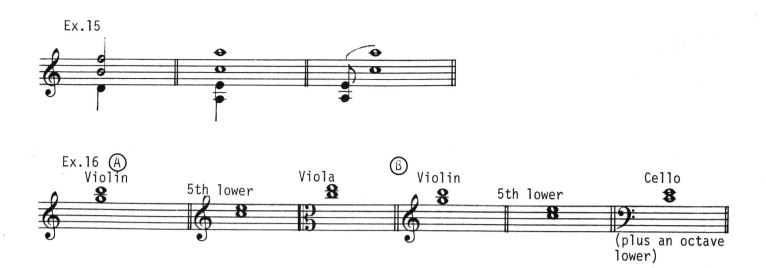

The strings may be considered — violin; (soprano with higher range) viola; (tenor range plus) cello; tenor (bass) and bass (bass).

Part IV

THE STRING ORCHESTRA

The string group contains all the members of the violin family—violins (1st and 2nds), violas, violoncellos, and double basses. This is the normal combination and any departures from it such as subdividing the groups, etc., are to be considered as being exceptions that require justification.

The strings are the most expressive department of the entire orchestra. They can play so quiet that the sound is hardly more than a whisper; they are also capable of playing with the utmost vigor and "brassiness." Many degrees of tonal contrast are possible through the use of the mute, picking (pizzicate) instead of bowing, tremolo, col legno (playing with the back of the bow), etc.

The 1st violins are the strongest because of their importance in the melodic and harmonic scheme. Furthermore, there is usually an extra desk of 1st violins available and they have a more powerful tone than 2nd violins. The 2nd violins and violas play a subordinate part and are therefore not so emphatic. The violoncellos and double basses are heard quite distinctly and in most cases are assigned to playing the bass line in octaves.

The string group is capable of playing any manner of passage, rapid or interrupted, diatonic or chromatic. They sustain tones easily and can play chords of two, three or four tones. They have an extreme variety of expression. The piano sketch of "America" (Ex. 17) is to be used as a model for all of the orchestrational sketches for strings.

Ex.17

The general lay-out for the string orchestra is in four part harmony:
VIOLINS I — VIOLINS II — VIOLAS — CELLI — STRING BASS

The bass doubles the cello at the lower octave *most* of the time. However, it is not to be inferred that they are at all times doubled in octaves. When the cello is playing solo or counterpoint, or an important figuration, the bass is placed on an independent line, if written high enough to be of determinate pitch; or on pedal-point; or, *tacet.*

Ex. 18 A shows "America" as written for the string quartet. Ex. 18Ⓑ: for the string orchestra.

Ex.18 Ⓐ

Violin 1

Violin 2

Viola

Cello

Ⓑ

Bass

Bass added for full String Orchestra

Assignment

Complete the arrangement of "America" as begun in Ex. 18Ⓐ and 18Ⓑ.

In Ex. 19 six voices are produced by doubling the top voice at the upper octave. Complete this arrangement.

Duplication of the parts of good harmony will produce, as demonstrated, consecutive octaves and 5ths. This is characteristic of this type of *block-harmony*, and serves to provide greater freedom from the rules of the strict choral and contrapuntal part writing. This idiom should be accepted and established as it will be met with many times, especially in modern music. The usual four part outline is shown in Ex. 20 Ⓐ. Duplication of the three upper voices in Ex. 20 Ⓑ. The parallel octaves and the 5ths are of course not objectionable.

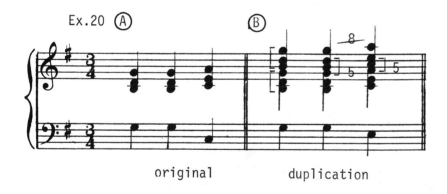

original   duplication

Ex. 21Ⓐ shows four part harmony. This is increased to six parts by duplicating the bass at the lower octave and the top voice at the upper octave (Ex. 21 Ⓑ).

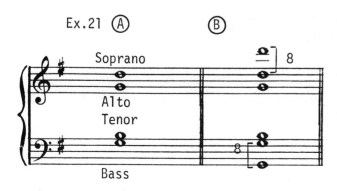

Ex. 22 Ⓐ provides eight voices by doubling the bass at the lower octave, the soprano and alto at the upper octave, and the tenor voice duplicated an octave higher. Ex. 22 Ⓑ provides nine voices by doubling the three upper voices at the upper octave, the bass at the lower octave and the soprano (melody) an octave lower. However, when the melody is doubled at the octave lower, it should not cause confusion with the bass part.

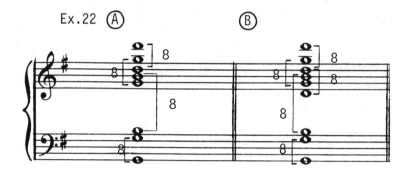

Ex. 23 shows the three upper voices doubled at the upper octave and the bass duplicated at the lower octave. Complete this arrangement.

Violins I, II and Viola are marked "divisi." This means literally "divided" and so one half of each group will play the top line of its part and the other half will play the bottom line.

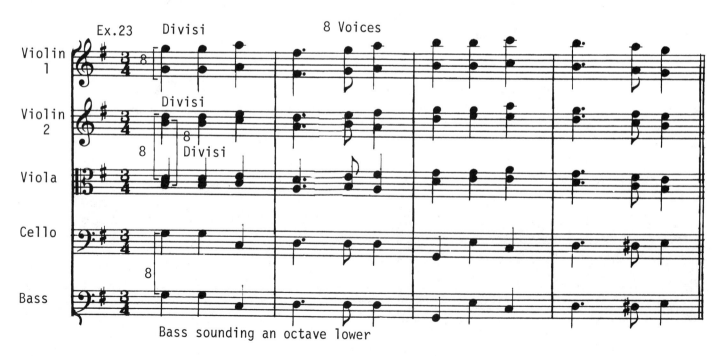

Bass sounding an octave lower

Complete the arrangement of "America" as begun in Ex. 24. Notice that the Violins I, II and the Violas are playing divisi. The melody in this case has been doubled at the lower octave and assigned to Cello I. The Cello II is on the bass part with the bass at the lower octave. Also, select any hymn-like composition and score it for string orchestra of 8 or 9 parts.

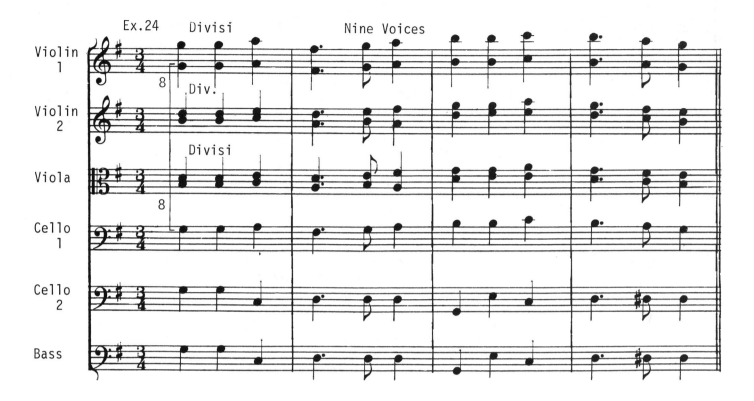

THE NON-HARMONIC ELEMENTS

Although this is not a text on harmony, there is an important harmonic consideration that must be established before any effective orchestration can be produced.

In treating ordinary four part harmony, the medium used as a rule is the piano or the quartet of human voices, etc. The tone color in these cases is the same and so much more care must be exercised in using the notes that pass through the harmony. However, in the orchestra, the tone color contrast between the different groups of instruments allows considerable freedom in respect to the use of passing tones, neighboring tones, suspensions, anticipation, pedal point, etc. These two simple principles will supply the brilliance that is often lacking in many orchestrations.

1. The basic harmony is never affected by the non-harmonic elements that pass through, above or below it.
2. The use of different tone colors will prevent any "seeming" harshness. See Ex. 25 Ⓐ, Ⓑ, and Ⓒ which illustrate the above.

Pedal point designs are more effective in the orchestra than in chamber music, or in piano, etc., because of the greater difference of tone color. See Ex. 26 Ⓐ, Ⓑ.

A melodic motive and its embellished form may be used simultaneously when different tone colors are in use (Ex. 26 Ⓒ).

Ex.26 Ⓐ

Ⓑ

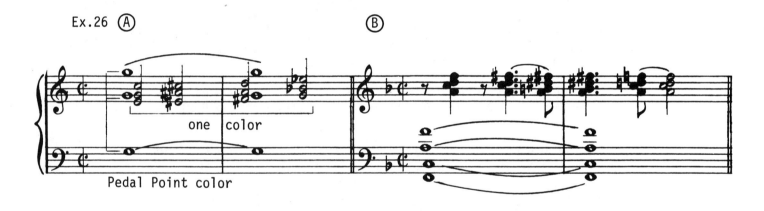

Ⓒ

There are two rules that will prevent the condition of writing "thin" scores; and what is equally poor, the writing of "thick" scores.

1. When writing from a piano part in which the hands are spaced far apart, fill in the space in your arrangement.
2. When thick chords are in the low register, rearrange them in open voicing, with a clear octave at the bottom.

The main consideration is in adapting the character of the original composition to the instrumental set-up. The arrangement should not sound like an arrangement at all but like a composition with good continuity. It is permissible to change the "letter" of the original so as to have good orchestration. This is good so long as the *character* is maintained.

Three and four part chords are best used in a continuity of marked, detached chords in *f* or *ff*.

In Ex. 27 Ⓐ, the original voicing of the piano chords has been changed. The chord in the first measure would sound thin if given to the strings as in the original; and the chord in the 3rd measure would sound muddy if voiced as written (Ex. 27 Ⓐ and Ⓑ).

ARPEGGIO AND PEDAL TREATMENT

The cello and bass are assigned to reproducing the effect of the sustaining pedal of the piano. The cello sustains the tones, while the bass gives the effect of striking the tones.

The melody is assigned to Violin I; the arpeggio is assigned to Viola and Violin II so as to insure smoothness and to prevent thinness of the inner voices. (See Ex. 28 Ⓐ, Ⓑ.)

Rapid broken chords are difficult on the strings, whereas they are extremely simple on the keyboard.

It is to be understood that in rapid, broken, angular chords, it is the *rhythm* that is important and *not* the outline of the arpeggio. However, a characteristic rhythm must be present in at least one part. The piano part of Ex. 29 Ⓐ has been translated into the string idiom. The broken 16ths of the piano become repeated 16ths for strings. The violas play the same notes an octave lower as the 2nd violins, thereby filling out the middle area. (See Ex. 29 Ⓐ, Ⓑ.)

BOWINGS

The bowings may be placed into two divisions:

1. The manner in which the bow is applied to the strings; or the way in which the player's individual style is expressed.
2. The particular directions which describe the type of bowing desired by the arranger.

The arrangement should always provide the bowing descriptions that are necessary for the correct interpretation of the phrase. The various bowings are as follows: They are the same in every particular for violin, viola, cello and string bass.

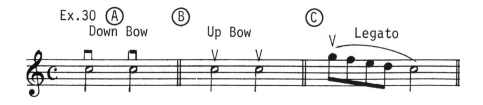

Detached (*marcato*) long down and up bows ⊓ ∨ ⊓ ∨ . The bow does not leave the strings. This type is for vigorous articulation. The notes may have dots over them or not. This type may be played in rapid tempo but as the speed is increased, the playing becomes more difficult (Ex. 31 Ⓐ, Ⓑ, Ⓒ, Ⓓ).

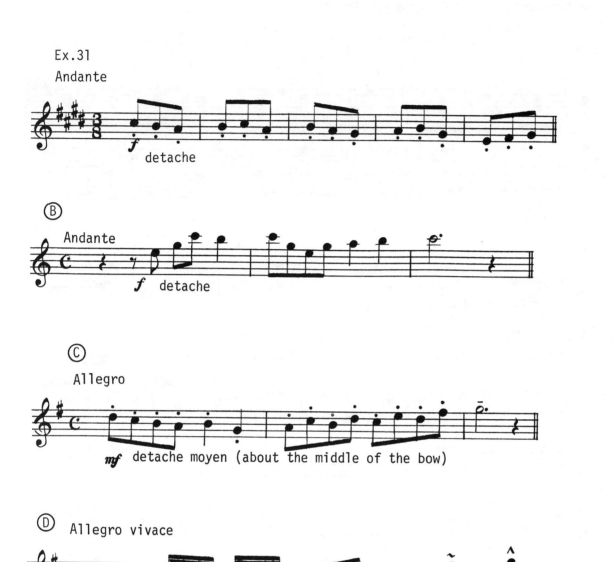

Ex.31
Andante

detache

Ⓑ
Andante

detache

Ⓒ
Allegro

detache moyen (about the middle of the bow)

Ⓓ Allegro vivace

petit detache (tip of the bow)

The down-bow is very strong, even violent. If this effect (vigorous) is desired, the bow is lifted for each note and attacked at the heel (bottom) of the bow. The recurrence of the attacks is limited (Ex. 32).

Ex.32

Allegro

MARTELE (Martellato)

This is a sharp, hammer-like blow of the very top of the bow, quick and hard. The dynamic range is large—from *p* to *f*. The effect is indicated by comma-like strokes above the notes, ⌄ ⌄ ⌄ and the words *a punta d'arco* added (Ex. 33 Ⓐ).

Another variation of this effect (martele) is very strong and is made with the heel of the bow instead of the tip. This effect is indicated by strokes below the notes—and the addition of the words *martele du talon* or just *du talon* (Ex. 33 Ⓑ).

Sautille (spiccato, saltando, saltato) is a springing bow (middle of bow) very light and fast (Ex. 34 Ⓐ).

THE JETE (Jumping Bow)

This effect is produced by throwing a down-bow upon the strings, picking up groups of notes without changing the direction of the bow (Ex. 34 Ⓑ).

STACCATO

Staccato shown here is an *up-bow* movement (from the tip to the middle of the bow) which takes up a rapid series of separated notes. This effect is very difficult and *not* advised in orchestral arranging. It is definitely a solo device. The notation is a slur which includes the whole group and a dot over each note (Ex. 35).

STACCATO

The notation is like that of the *staccato* itself but is confined to *small* groups of notes, either slow or rapid. The up-bow is preferred for this type of staccato because it is not adaptable to forte passages (Ex. 36).

Another type of orchestral *staccato* is that of groups of two notes of which the second note is shorted and *not* accented. The bowing signs may be different for these groups but one definite principle covers all of them, i.e., the first note of the two is definitely shorter but never the second note of the pair and both are played without changing the bow's direction (Ex. 37 Ⓐ, Ⓑ, Ⓒ, Ⓓ, Ⓔ).

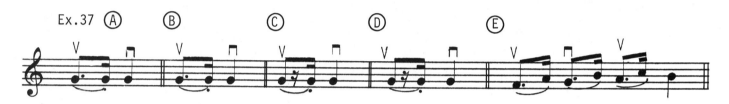

LOURE

This effect is for cantabile passages (song-like designs) and is expressed by a slur covering the passage to be played under one bow and a dash above every note. The bow receives much pressure on the notes with a slight pause after it. Inasmuch as the notes require strong bowing, it is advisable to limit the groups to two, three or four notes.

EXACT TREMOLO

The rapid repetition of a note (or two notes) by causing the bow to be played back and forth across the string (or strings) (Ex. 39 Ⓐ, Ⓑ).

BOWED TREMOLO

This is an orchestral device and calls for the extreme repetition of the note (or notes). The notation is three or four strokes across the stem of the note and with the addition of the term "tremolo" so as to insure proper interpretation (Ex. 40 Ⓐ, Ⓑ).

THE FINGERED (Slurred) TREMOLO

In this effect, the bow moves continuously on *one* string (not strings) and the fingers produce the resulting sound (very much as in the trill). The interval is a 3rd, 4th or at the most, diminished 5th, all of which must be played upon the same string. On the viola the perfect 4th and on the cello the major 3rd should be utmost limits of the fingered tremolo.

Special attention should be given to the notation that was required of the bowed tremolo. The time value of each pair of voices must be considered (Ex. 41 Ⓐ, Ⓑ, Ⓒ).

PIZZACATO

This device is indicated as *pizz.* In this case the bow is not used and the string is "picked" by the finger. The bow is held in the hand and a little time must be given so that the bow can be brought into position again.

The small notes should be used only when doubled with the woodwinds; by themselves they are without resonance.

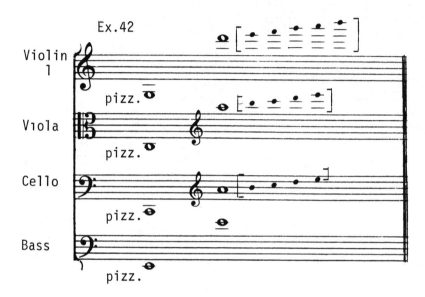

OTHER DEVICES IN USE FOR STRINGS

THE MUTE
(SORDINO, SOURDINE, DÄMPFER)

This is a device that is placed upon the bridge to reduce the volume of tone and is conducive to mysterious or veiled backgrounds.

COL LEGNO

This effect indicates using the back of the bow (the wood). It is not used in conventional music as the tone is dry, brittle and harsh.

SUL PONTICELLO

This means to play closely to the bridge and the result is a discordant brittle tone. It is not a very popular effect for normal usage.

SUL TASTO

Played with the bow over the fingerboard.

Part V

WOOD WINDS and HORNS

These instruments may be arranged as an independent choir and this idea will be established after first showing the manner in which chords are "voiced" for the group.

When instruments of different timbres are used in combination, they should be "dove-tailed" in order to have a good blend. Such a treatment is shown in Ex. 43.

There are cases where this effect is impossible owing to the range of the instruments that are in use. In this next example, dove-tailing is not possible due to the low register of the oboe. The blending however, is acceptable because of the rich, thick reediness of the low clarinets (Ex. 44).

Ex.43   Ex.44

The dove-tailing of flutes and oboes in a high register would *not* be recommended because it would place the first oboe in its thin shrill register (Ex. 45 Ⓐ).

The dove-tailing of low or middle register chords with flutes and oboes would result in placing the 2nd flute in its soft middle register where it could easily be absorbed by the other instruments (Ex. 45 Ⓑ). The proper scoring for Ex. 45 Ⓐ and Ⓑ is shown in Ex. 46 Ⓐ and Ⓑ. (The same conditions will be present if dove-tailing the clarinets and flutes.)

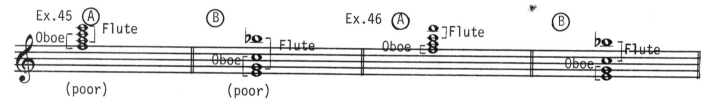

Ex. 47Ⓐ shows a quiet chord voiced for 2 each of wood wind and 2 horns in F. Each pair of wood-winds is dove-tailed except the flutes and there is an open octave at the bottom of the chord.

Ex. 47Ⓑ shows a loud chord. In this case, the clarinets are placed above the oboes so as to supply brilliance to the chords. (The oboe becomes impoverished in tone in its higher area but the clarinet attains power as it approaches its upper register.)

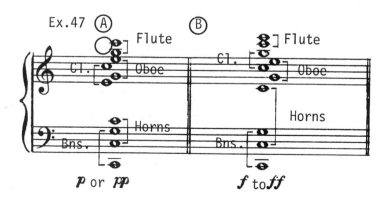

Dove-tailing is, of course, the best procedure for good sonority but do not lean over backward in attempting to apply the principle to all cases. There will be exceptions to this normal procedure as shown in Ex. 45Ⓐ and Ⓑ.

In laying out the tones of a chord, follow the normal order of the harmonic series, i.e., wide spaces in the lower register with the intervals coming closer and closer together as they approach the upper register. Also to obtain good depth and resonance, be sure that there is an open octave at the bottom of the chord (at least).

The following phrases will serve as models for scoring for the wood winds and horns.

Ex. 48 shows an imitation technique with the imitations assigned judicially to the instruments best able to play them in the designated registers. In the 2nd measure the flutes and 2nd oboe are dove-tailed; in the 3rd measure the clarinets and 2nd horn are dove-tailed; in the 5th measure, the bassoons and 2nd horn are dove-tailed; in the 7th and 8th measures there is no dove-tailing because of the difference in registers of the instruments involved.

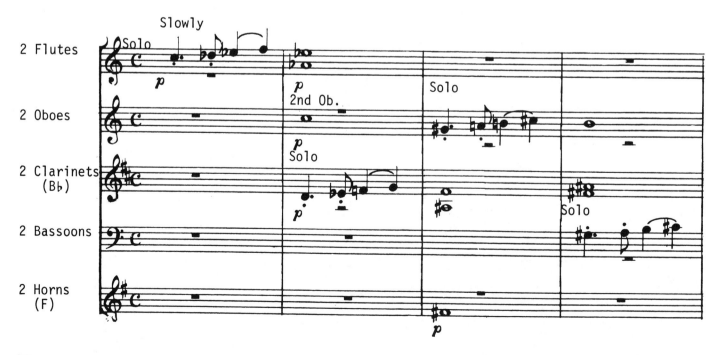

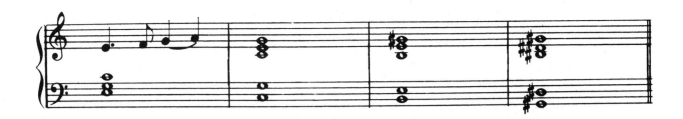

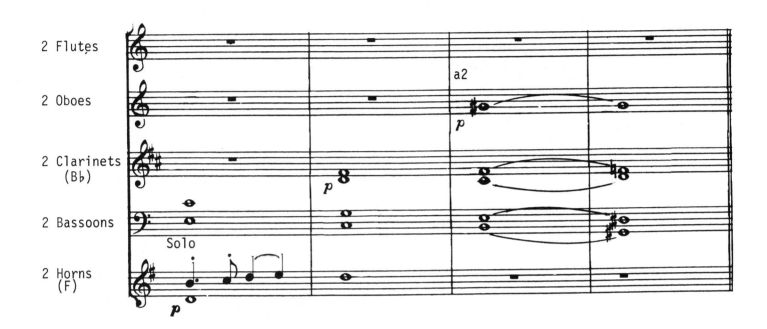

Ex. 49 shows the melody (in tenor range) assigned to the 1st horn with the flute taking the embellishments above and bassoons on sustained tones. The oboe enters with the solo at the 3rd measure. The clarinet enters with solo in the 4th measure so as to cope with the low notes of the melody. The 1st bassoon takes the solo in the 5th measure with accompanying parts in flute and 2nd bassoon.

Assignment

Orchestrate for 2 flutes — 2 oboes (one oboe, one English horn) — 2 clarinets — 2 bassoons — 2 horns in F any desired composition of similar nature. Also arrange "America" for wood winds and horns.

Ex. 50 shows that the 1st and 2nd measures are so different in register that they require contrasting types of instruments to those that would be used at measure 3 and 4. In the 3rd and 4th measures the 1st horn has the melody with the 2nd horn, 2 bassoons and 2 clarinets completing the harmony. The two horns and bassoons resemble four horns when used in this manner. The flutes might just as well have been left out of the 1st two measures but playing as they do at the upper octave, they will add brightness and good contrast to the next two measures.

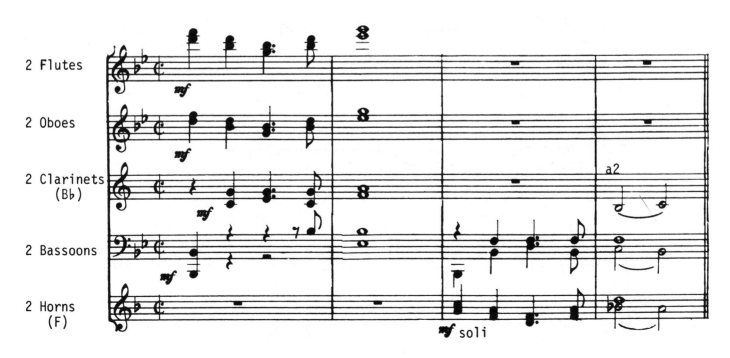

COMBINATION OF TRUMPETS, TROMBONES and HORNS

The four horns are capable of producing four part harmony, well balanced in tone (Ex. 51).

When the bass is doubled in octaves, the third trombone and tuba are used in octaves while the three upper parts are given to trombones I and II, reinforced by a trumpet or two horns in unison (Ex. 52).

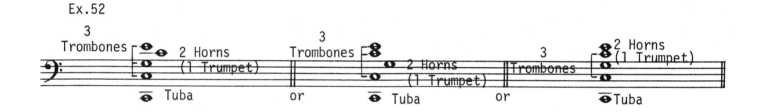

A fine combination is — 2 horns and tuba forming the bass in octaves, with the three trombones playing the other three parts (Ex. 53 Ⓐ).

When the chord is in a high register, the two upper voices are given to the two trumpets and the two lower voices to the two trombones or to four horns in pairs (Ex. 53 Ⓑ).

When three trumpets are in use the fourth part may be given to a trombone or to two horns in unison (Ex. 54 Ⓐ).

Dove-tailing of parts is always in order between instruments of different texture (Ex. 54 Ⓑ).

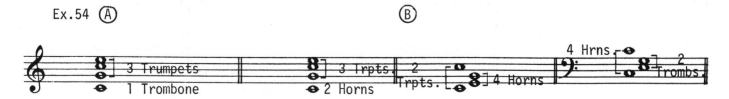

The same principle holds good during chord progression (Ex. 55).

Ex.55

With three-tone chords, the best arrangement is to have horns, trumpets or trombones in threes. If used in combination, the number of horns should be doubled to preserve the balance (Ex. 56).

Ex.56

When all groups are used the number of horns should be doubled (Ex. 57).

Ex.57

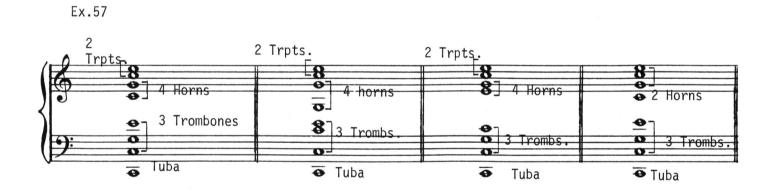

In harmony of five or more voices, certain voices must be left out (Ex. 58 and 59).

Ex.58

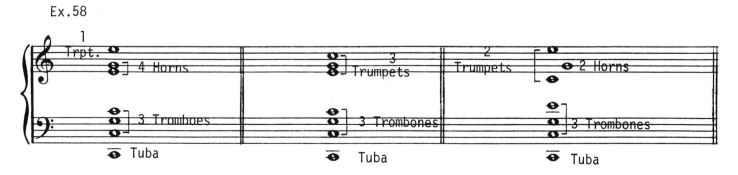

Ex.59

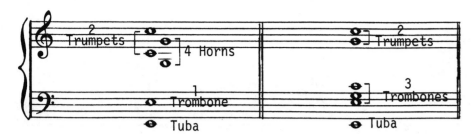

Intervals of the 2nd, 7th, 9th, etc., are better given to instruments of different tone color (Ex. 60 Ⓐ).

When only two trumpets are in use, the horns cannot move in pairs, but the effect will sound well if the horns are marked a dynamic degree more than the others. This will insure good balance (Ex. 60 Ⓑ).

Ex.60 Ⓐ   Ⓑ

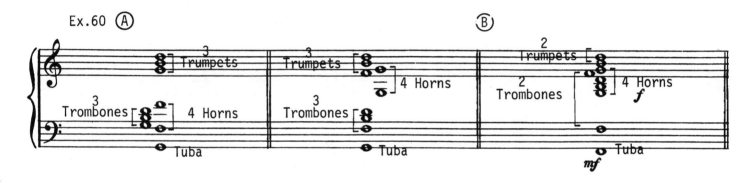

The same principle prevails when horns in pairs would be too weak to balance. When the chord covers a large compass, the horns are not necessarily doubled (Ex. 61).

Ex.61

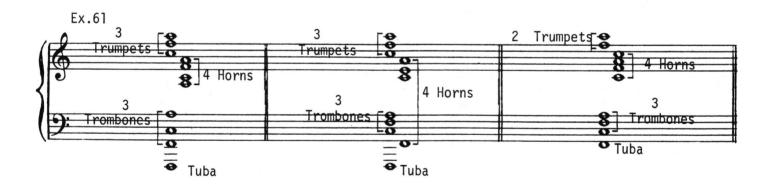

Very often the horns are played directly alongside trumpets or trombones. The soft tone of the horns add roundness to the brassy tones of the trumpet and trombone (Ex. 62).

Ex.62

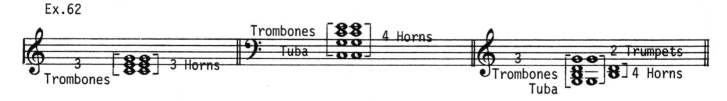

Trombones and trumpets side by side are not commonly used (Ex. 63).

The brass is often used to sustain tones in two or more octaves (Ex. 64).

N.B. In scoring loud passages for brass, remember that the horns are about one-half as strong so that two horns are needed to balance one trumpet or one trombone. However, in quiet passages all are of equal force.

Assignment

Score for 2 trumpets in Bb — 2 tenor trombones; 1 bass trombone; 1 tuba; 4 french horns in F:

1. "Onward Christian Soldiers" (or any other similar hymn or chorale)
2. "America"
3. Using the same scoring, orchestrate Ex. 65 with the Flute as solo.

Part VI

FULL ENSEMBLE

SUGGESTIONS FOR SCORING

Every composition presents its own problems and it is not possible to provide a definite formula that will meet with every contingency. In orchestration, as in composition, it is only the technique that can be learned from books or from a teacher. The application of the devices depend on the musicianship, experience, imagination and common sense of the writer. However, there are certain common faults that can be guarded against and other treatments that are more or less standard:

1. Avoid the "Sectional" effect, i.e., a part for strings alone, followed by a part for w.w. alone, then brass alone, then strings alone again. This is sometimes possible if the character of the piece warrants it; but in general a blending of the various groups makes for better continuity.

2. Avoid thickness, this is caused by the low spacing of harmony. Wide spacing is desirable for lower registers. It is also caused by the desire to give instruments something to do. Do not have instruments wandering aimlessly. If not needed to give weight or point to a passage, they are better left tacet.

3. Avoid thinness, which is caused by wide spacing of harmony in middle area. A single horn is sufficient to fill such gaps, and to give body to the chord.

4. Do not overwork the horns. The use of horns is sure to prevent thinness in the middle octaves of the orchestra, but their continuous use becomes monotonous and tiring to the players.

5. Reserve high tones (extreme) on brass and w.w. for loud climaxes.

6. Do not use the brass and percussion merely for noise. They may often be used quietly with good effect.

7. The strings are the backbone of the orchestra and may be used for long passages. The ear does not tire of the string tone. In quiet passages use divisi instead of double stops. In passages of a forceful nature, double stops are good especially in 2nd violins and violas. Make sure that they are easy to play.

8. In vocal accompaniments, keep the background transparent so as to let the voice through. The safest rule is to rely on the strings and to keep the w.w. soft. Use the brass for accents and open spaces where "fill-in" figurations are desirable. *(NO melody in orchestra.)*

9. No important tone should be left out of brass. Have good balance.

10. The w.w. can only double the brass. Unison doublings are not of much account except for oboe doubling trumpet in middle register; clarinet above the staff with high trumpet (in unison).

11. The other w.w. at upper level for flute, clarinets, piccolo, bassoons and bass clarinet in low register.

12. The strings are placed in their normal registers. The best layout for the full symphony orchestra is shown in Ex. 66.

Ex.66

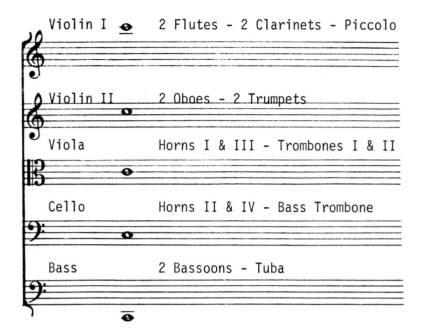

Keep the structure simple. Don't overload. Independent parts may muddle clarity of sound; doubling is therefore necessary for ensemble effect (see Ex. 67 — sounds as written). Score similarly Ex. 68, 69, 70.

Treatment of a strong melodic line on top with chords sustained, or detached, below it (Ex. 68).

In the example given, the melody must stand out with power and clarity in the arrangement, and apparently calls for a great sweep of strings. The chords in the left hand may be extended upward and so be suitable for all of the brass. To reproduce the slurring of the chords onto the octave "C" on the 3rd beat of the measure (a pianistic effect), the chords must be tied over an eighth note with the bassoons, tuba, string bass and timpani supplying the octave "C."

90

The w.w. with the exception of the bassoon, are used to reinforce the strings. Proper balance demands that more w.w. should double the top line of the melody than those that double the other two octaves. The melody is arranged in three octaves instead of two for greater breadth and sonority.

If the same melody was arranged in two octaves, all of the violins would play the top octave, whereas the viola and cellos would play the lower octave. There would be no need of the wood winds doubling in this case. They would then be used to double the brass.

In Ex. 68 there is a mass of sustained harmony that requires a powerful melodic line to cut through it; that is why much doubling is done by the w.w. However, if the accompanying chords are detached, it is not necessary to reinforce the strings with the wood winds.

A few other powerful melodic combinations for this type of rochestration are:

1. Top Octave: 1 and 2 violins; flutes and clarinets.
    Lower Octave: 2 trumpets and oboes.

2. Top Octave: 2 trumpets.
    Lower Octave: 2 or 3 trombones or 4 horns.

3. Violas, 1 trumpet and all upper w.w. in unison, not octaves.

4. The instruments in 3, on the upper octave. Cellos and 4 horns on lower.

MELODIC LINES IN THE MIDDLE

Ex. 69 (A) shows the melodic line in the middle with the accompaniment above and below. This case is actually "3" part counterpoint with the melody (C.F.) in the middle and the counterpoint above and below. The counterpoint above is in "4" part harmony with the flutes and 1st violins playing the top line, clarinets and oboes dove-tailed, playing the inner parts, trumpets and 2nd violins playing as the flutes and 1st violins but an octave lower.

As the melody (C.F.) is in the middle, it should be very powerful to cut through the mass of harmony above and the counter melody below. Therefore, in order to arrive at this effect, we use the violas, cellos, English horns and 4 French horns (horns in "F") in unison. For the bottom line, we use the basses, bassoons, bass clarinet, tuba and trombone. Timpani is used sparingly in passages such as these on the tonic and the 5th. This combination balances the orchestra beautifully.

Passages for bass parts like this have to be shared between trombones as in Ex. 69 (B). The three trombones are then only equal to one trombone and so the bass line is not as heavy as it might appear to be. The tuba can play the whole passage alone in the bottom octave of course. (This example should be written out in full score for practice [Ex. 69 (B)].)

TREATMENT OF A PRINCIPAL MELODIC LINE IN BASS

The analysis of Ex. 70 should make the procedure easily managed. Where there is no important inner line, the cellos are available for the bass part. Also the violas and horns where the range is suitable. The trombones are used only when the bass part is adaptable for them. Otherwise, they are better used if filling in the harmony, or emphasizing with the *sfz.* They are often used (as in Ex. 70) in outlining a bass part which is being played in its entirety by the more agile instruments.

Attention is called to the adjustment for the w.w. Rapid reiteration is not easy on single reed instruments but with the treatment illustrated for clarinets and bassoons, the effect will sound smoothly. Notice also that the horns are staggered.

COMBINATION OF WOOD-WINDS AND HORNS

Two or more instruments may be combined in the octave, double-octave or unison. These combinations may be regarded as composite colors. The octave combinations are regarded as being more useful and effective than the unison combination. In any case, however, the unisons are used freely. The following chart will prove useful in deciding the different tone-blendings that are available.

Instruments	Unison	Octaves
2 Flutes, or any 2 instruments of the same color	Adds strength, but no new color. Solo better for individuality.	Not recommended, as the strong and weak registers are combined.
Flute / Oboe	Good.	Fine sonority, and better than unison. Adds brightness.
Flute / Horn	Good (low flute).	Good.
Flute / Clarinet	Good in all possible registers.	Adds brilliance.
Flute / Bassoon	Flute must be in low register and bassoon in high register.	Adds brightness; excellent at double octave.
Oboe / Clarinet	Intense. Good in small doses.	Only when the Clarinet is in low register.
Oboe / Horn	Not good; the blend is not satisfactory.	Excellent.
Oboe / Bassoon	Good, but very reedy.	Excellent.
Clarinet / Bassoon	Good; rich.	Very good; also at double octave.
Clarinet / Horn	Very good blend.	. . . .
Bassoon / Horn	Very good blend; does not affect the horn quality.	Good blend.
Flutes / Oboes / Clarinets	Uniform tone, and very powerful.	Good, especially in three registers.
Clarinets / Bassoon / Horns	Rich; powerful.	Clarinets above Horns and Bassoons.

A passage is marked as solo when only one player has the melody or counter-melody; when two or more players are used on a passage, use the plural term—soli.

When two instruments are used on the same line in unison the part is marked a2. If three players are used on a part, in unison, the part is marked a3.

There should be a few measures rest before a solo enters, so that the new voice will attract the necessary attention.

WOOD-WINDS — HORNS — STRINGS

Tone Color Combinations

Instruments	In the Unison	In the Octave
Violins / Oboes	Not recommended, unless there are many violins. But if used, *ff* is best.	Oboe at upper octave of low violins.
Violins / Flutes	Good effect in *p* or *pp* Not in *f* or *f*	One or two flutes octave above violins.
Violins / Clarinets	Good blend with low violins and clarinets.	Good when violins are above clarinets.
Violin / Bassoon	Excellent at low registers of violin.	Good with violin at upper octave.
Violin / Horn	Good, in best registers of horn.	Not advised in open sound. When both are muted the effect is good, more so when violin is above.
Violas / Clarinets	Excellent when clarinets are in low register.	Good.
Violas / Flutes	Good.	Flute above.
Violas / Oboes	Oboe in unison with high viola aids piercing quality.	Oboe above.
Cellos / Bassoons	Smooth and full.	. . . .
Cellos / Horns	Best in tenor range at all dynamic levels.	. . . .
Cellos / Oboes	Good, especially with high register of cello.	Good in *p*, with oboe above.
Cellos / Flutes or Clarinets	Possible in available registers.	Octaves not good as a blend.
Double-bass / Bassoons	Good, when the cellos are busy on another line.	Bassoon at upper octave when the cellos are busy on another line.

Part VII

BIG BAND ARRANGING

In the modern big band, there is greater freedom of movement than in the symphony orchestra because of its limitations of tonal resources.

The brass must adopt the use of different types of mutes which simulate various tone colors. For example, the French horn may be imitated by the trumpet or trombone by playing them in their medium registers in hats and marking "no vibrato." This will reproduce the open round sound of the French horn.

The oboe can be imitated by the trumpet in a very close mute such as the "cup mute" or the "Harmon mute with pipe."

The clarinet can be treated the same as in the symphony orchestra but it is noted that in big bands, it is particularly adapted to high, screaming melodic line also.

Other symphonic instruments may be imitated such as the bassoon by the tenor or baritone saxophone.

The flute and bass clarinet are treated much the same as in the symphony orchestra: Note however that the saxophone usually doubles on the bass clarinet and clarinet; some even double on the flute. However, when writing for a big band, it is wise to know exactly what instruments your musicians double on.

Violins are treated the same as in the symphony orchestra, bearing in mind, of course, that they must adapt the mood of the big band.

As discussed in symphonic orchestration, concerted harmony prevails throughout big band arranging.

THE SAXOPHONES

The usual set-up for the dance orchestra is: ALTO (lead), ALTO, TENOR, TENOR. If five saxes are used, the Baritone is added.

The Alto sax is written a major 6th above concert.

The Tenor sax is written a whole tone plus an octave above concert.

The Baritone sax is written a major 6th plus an octave above concert. (Same as alto, but an octave lower in sound.)

The Bb soprano is used for special effects and one of the players doubles on it. The part is written one whole tone above concert.

Ex. 1 shows the complete complass and practical range of the saxophones.
The same written range is used for all saxes.

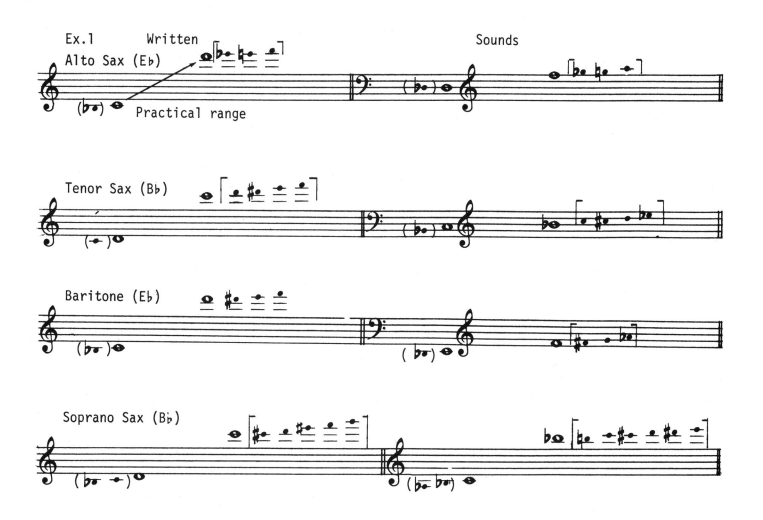

The use of "open" voicing is advocated today especially with tunes of a cantabile, ballad-like nature. The term "open" voicing means that the compass of the parts is more than an octave, i.e., from the lowest voice to the top voice. As shown in Ex. 2Ⓐ, the chord is first written in close position and then the tone below the lead is placed an octave lower. This manipulation will bring the chord into semi open position (Ex. 2Ⓐ).

Ex. 2Ⓑ shows a chord progression which was treated as in Ex. 2Ⓐ bringing the note below the lead an octave lower (Ex. 2Ⓑ).

Ex. 2Ⓒ shows the progression as written (and transposed) for the saxophones.

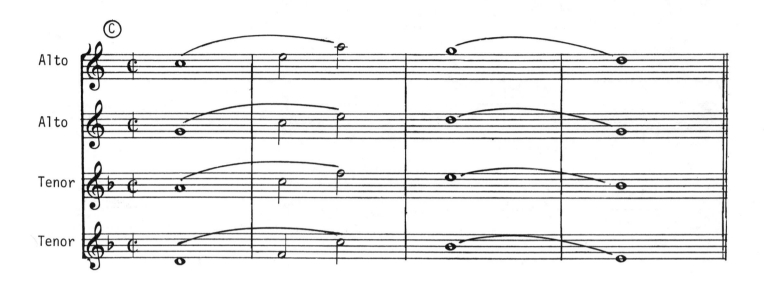

In symphonic orchestration the principles of dove-tailing were presented. This operation is suggested when low-voiced chords are in use in the saxophone section. The result will be a much clearer sonority (Ex. 3).

Ex.3

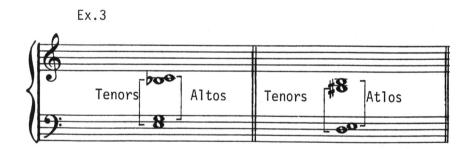

Also submitted in Symphonic Orchestra were the newer treatments of parallel, concerted voice-leading. However, it must be stated again that parallel writing is now only *allowed,* but in this type it is *necessary* so as to present the proper "idiom." In almost every case in "sectional" playing, the harmony voices follow the direction and the rhythm of the lead voice and so the conventional rules of voice-leading, as applied to the chorale types and similar designs are relinquished. In most of the examples submitted in this part of the work, such conditions will prevail. This will often result in 7th and 9ths and 11ths rising (instead of descending) but as previously stated, the lead voice and the other harmony voices will *pull* such tones along.

Ex. 4Ⓐ: Closed Harmony. Ⓑ: Semi-open Harmony. Ⓒ: Dove-tailed which gives very good sound in low register.

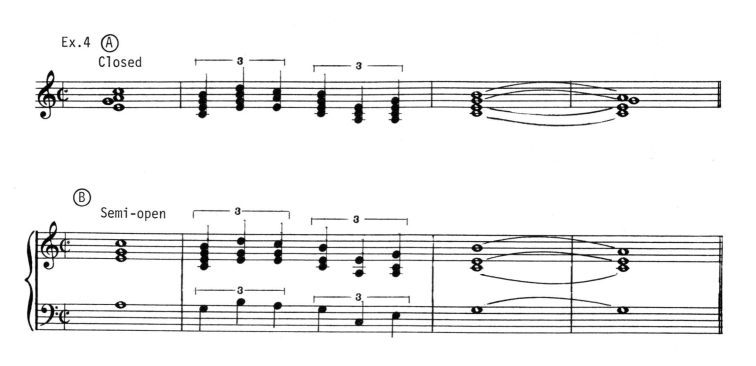

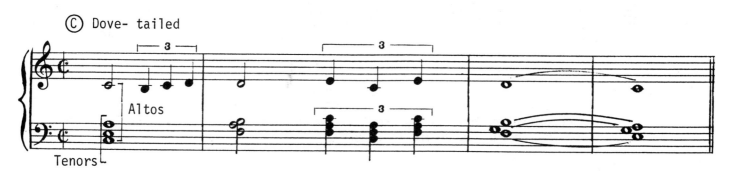

OPEN VOICING

In open voicing, the 2nd and 4th voices from the top are placed one octave lower (this voicing is best used in slow tempos) which gives a small orchestra a big sound. All voicings are interchangeable but it is best to make this change at some dynamic point (from ff to pp or vice versa or at the cadence break, etc.) in the arrangement (Ex. 5).

Ex.5
Open-voicing

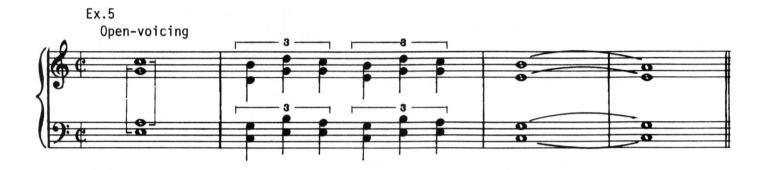

FIVE SAXOPHONES

4 part chords are to be used in *all* cases. 9th chords are to be used in incomplete form, i.e., 3rd, 5th, 7th and 9ths. The root being heard from the (baritone sax) chords with added 6th and 9th are to be written 3rd, 5th, 6th and 9th. 11th chords as 5th, 7th, 9th and 11th. 13th chords as 3rd, 7th, 9th and 13th. The baritone sax may be used on all root with these examples (Ex. 6).

Ex.6

Ex. 7 Ⓐ: 5 Saxes with lead doubled on 5th sax (baritone). Ⓑ: 5 Saxes in semi-open voicing with lead doubled 8*va* lower on 4th tenor sax. Ⓒ: 5 Saxes in open voicing with lead on 3rd tenor sax.

Ex.7 Ⓐ   Ⓑ   Ⓒ

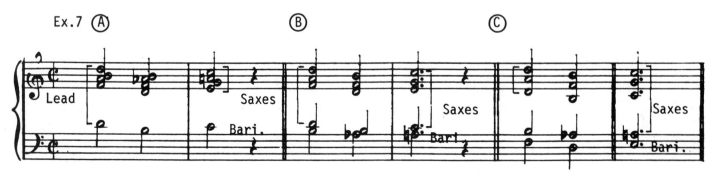

Ex. 8(A) is an example of 4-part harmony in semi-open voicing with baritone sax (5th sax) in the same rhythm but in contrary motion to the tones that it doubles. The baritone may also be used on all roots or sostenuto, etc. (Ex. 8 (B), (C), (D), (E)).

Five-part chord
at sustained point
allowed here.

Assignment

Transpose Ex. 3 to 8 to the proper keys for the altos, tenors and baritones. Also select any pop tune of the day and arrange it for 5 saxes as in the examples illustrated.

Clusters of 5-part harmony are useful for effect but in a more modern type of arranging. My advice to the beginner is to use them sparingly. They may be closed, semi-open or open (Ex. 9).

Ex.9

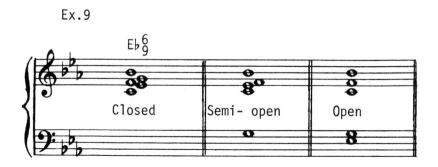

In regard to 2nds, they are to be avoided above the staff in ballad type tunes (Ex. 10 Ⓐ), but for swinging type tunes they are permissible (Ex. 10 Ⓑ). However, 2nds within the staff are harmless.

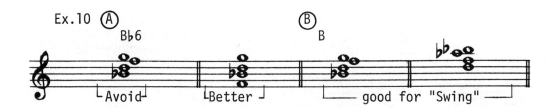

The five saxes in close harmony with high clarinet were introduced in the early '40s by Glenn Miller. It has been exploited to its fullest extent; however, the effect is sometimes good and it is entitled to consideration. The only condition is that the clarinet be placed into a register that will not take the lead tenor too high and also in such a register that will retain the brilliance of the clarinet. The sketch in Ex. 11Ⓐ shows the best range for the tenor sax and clarinet.

As mentioned in the musical Ex. 10Ⓐ and Ⓑ, if the tenor lead causes 2nds with the part above it, the effect is accepted because the lead tenor moves with "thematic authority." Ex. 11Ⓑ shows an additional example of this effect.

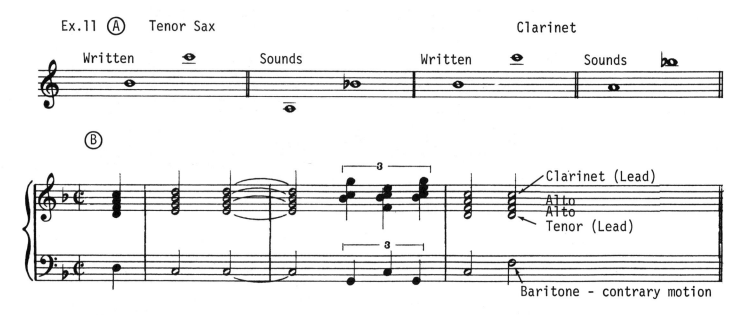

The following examples are taken from arrangements illustrating the various possibilities of the reed section.

Study minutely the exercises that follow and transpose the clarinets, altos, tenors and baritones in each exercise to their proper keys. Then you are to make up examples of your own using pop tunes or any tunes that you like.

Alto Solo

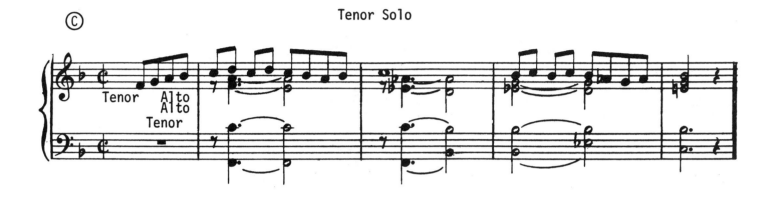

Tenor Solo

3 Altos - 2 Tenors
The 5th Alto is doubled by the Baritone

Ex. 12 Ⓕ is to be written in duet for two altos, two tenors and baritone on the melody, making a total of 3 octaves.

Ex. Ⓖ, Ⓗ, to be transposed to proper key for each instrument.

(Sounds as Written)

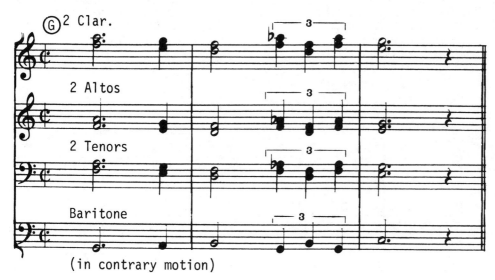

(in contrary motion)

SAXOPHONE TRILLS

There are some trills that are impossible on the saxophone and others that are very difficult. A good general principle is to avoid any trills that deal with the low note Bb, B♮, C and C♯. Also, rapid figures that revolve around these tones are dangerous. However, passages and arpeggios that pass through them are permissible (Ex. 13 Ⓐ, Ⓑ, Ⓒ).

Ex.13 Ⓐ   Ⓑ   Ⓒ

THE BRASS

When there are 4 or 5 brass, they should be voiced in 4-part harmony like the saxes. All of the examples of Ex. 12 in closed or open harmony with solors in 3rds are available for the brass. If the example is too low for the brass, transpose upwards. When in 4-part harmony, use 3 trumpets and 2 trombones; where there are solos, give the solos to the 1st trumpet and harmony to the remaining instruments, etc.

Ex. 14 Ⓐ: Voicing 2 trumpets and 1 trombone. Ⓑ: 3 trumpets and 1 trombone. Ⓒ: 3 trumpets and 2 trombones. Ⓓ: 3 trumpets and 3 trombones.

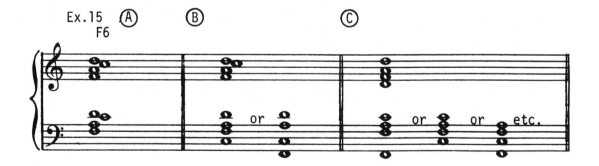

When writing for 4 trumpets and 4 trombones (8 brass), write the trombones exactly as the trumpets but an *8va* lower. Ex. 15 Ⓐ: 8 brass. Ⓑ: 8 brass with trombones open. Ⓒ: 8 brass semi-open.

Assignment

Transpose all of the examples in Ex. 12 for the brass. Also select any tunes that you like and arrange them for 8 brass.

As previously outlined, the use of mutes for the brass create many effective colors and blends. The mutes in use are: straight mute, Harmon mute, cup mute and Harmon mute with "pipe." There is also the Plunger and the Hat. Some combinations are good such as the Harmon mute in Hat, straight mute in Hat, etc., but with practice, one begins to create his own effects. My advice to you is to listen to the brass with the use of each type of mute to get acquainted with their sounds. These mutes are available for both trumpets and trombones. Ex. 16 Ⓐ, Ⓑ, Ⓒ show some of the voicings for 4 trumpets (also with the use of the mute). Ex. 16 Ⓓ, Ⓔ, Ⓕ show voicing for 4 trombones (also with mutes).

4 Trumpets - with Cup Mutes

4 Trumpets - Hat Mute

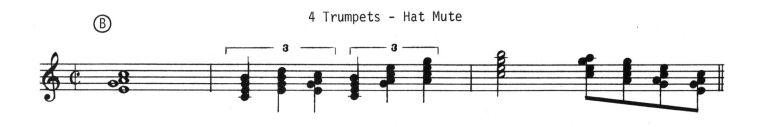

Solo Trumpet

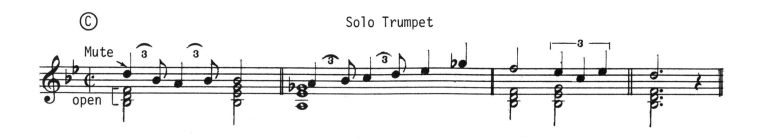

4 Trombones - Open

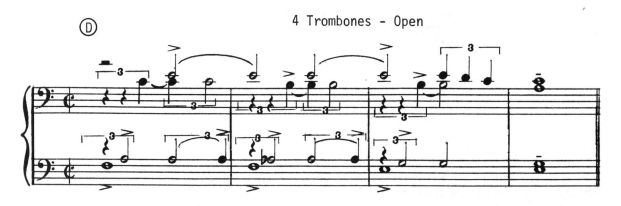

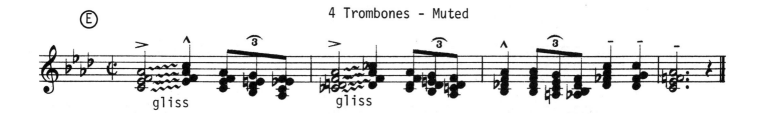

4 Trombones - Muted

gliss   gliss

Solo Trombone - Muted

Mute

open

THE RHYTHM SECTION

The rhythm consists of the piano, drums, bass and guitar and their treatments is as follows: The piano presents the harmonic structure with the right hand, which is written in the treble clef and the bass tone with the left hand which is written in the bass clef. This in itself embraces the entire harmonic structure of a composition. It is recommended that four note chords be written for the right hand so that the player may see at a glance the harmonic design. Ex. 17Ⓐ shows the best compass for the right hand. Ex. 17Ⓑ shows the best compass for the left hand and it should not conflict with the lowest tones of the right hand.

The double bass part duplicates the piano bass part (Ex. 17Ⓒ).

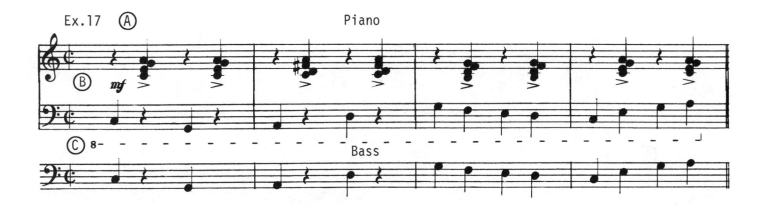

The DRUMS: The snare drum is written on the 3rd space in the bass clef and the bass drum is written on the first space. The drummers responsibilities should be indicated. Ex. 18 Ⓐ, Ⓑ, Ⓒ, Ⓓ show some of the more conventional treatments.

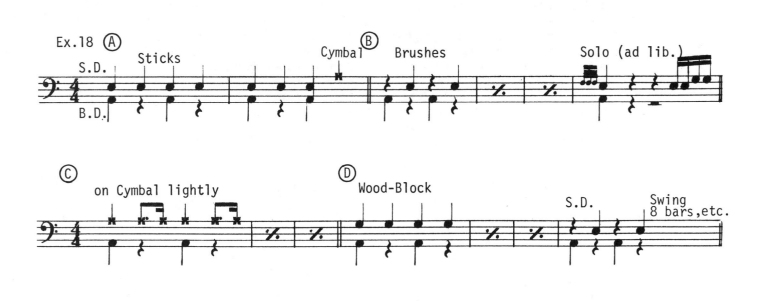

The GUITAR is tuned upward from E to A, D, G, B, and E.

These tones sound one octave lower than written. Ex. 19 Ⓐ, Ⓑ. Chord symbols are written for the guitar and the modern guitarist plays three and four note chords. The old style playing of full six string chords across the instrument is no longer in use (except in rock 'n roll music and rhythm and blues where only major and minor triads are used). One simply names the chord structure with the necessary time values in the staff and the player will do the rest (Ex. 19 Ⓒ).

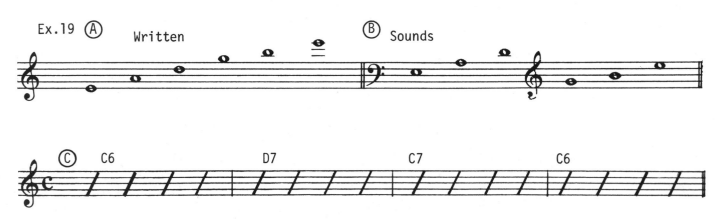

ENSEMBLE WITH CONCERTED RHYTHM

COMBINATION 1.

1st trumpet
2nd trumpet — 1st alto *8va* lower
3rd trumpet — 2nd alto   "   "
1st trombone — 1st tenor "   "
2nd trombone — 2nd tenor on lead, an octave below 1st trumpet. *Baritone, independent.* This type of arrangement is used for vaudeville acts and the saxes overlap the brass. This is done to insure a good sound with either large or small orchestra. When writing this type of arrangement, always cue in the melody on the *piano part.*

COMBINATION 2.

1st trumpet — lead
2nd trumpet —
3rd trumpet —
1st trombone —
2nd trombone — lead
1st alto — lead, octave lower than 1st trumpet
2nd alto — as 2nd trumpet. "8va" lower
1st tenot — as 3rd trumpet. "8va" lower
2nd tenor — as 1st trombone. "8va" lower
baritone — as 2nd trombone. "8va" lower

The above combination must be placed in a high key so as to enable the 1st alto sax to play in a good register.

COMBINATION 3.

1st trumpet —
2nd trumpet —
3rd trumpet — as first alto. "8va" lower
1st trombone — as 3rd alto. "8va" lower
2nd trombone — as 1st tenor. "8va" lower
2nd tenor — as 2nd trumpet an octave lower
Baritone — as 3rd trumpet or an independent line

The following combinations are not in concerted rhythm.

COMBINATION 4

Trumpets 1, 2, 3 in trio harmony, soli with muted trombones and saxes in background as follows:

1st alto
2nd alto
1st trombone
1st tenor
2nd trombone
2nd tenor
baritone   on sustained harmony

COMBINATION 5. Trumpets and trombones in soli. Saxophones as background playing in sustained harmony or figuration, or on counterpoint on unison or harmonization.

COMBINATION 6. Saxophones in soli. Trombones in background on sustained Harmony or figuration or on counterpoint.

COMBINATION 7. Saxophones on soli. Trumpets on sustained harmony, figuration or counterpoint.

COMBINATION 8. Trombones on soli. Saxes on sustained harmony, on figuration or counterpoint.

COMBINATION 9. Trombones on soli. Saxes and trumpets in background as described above.

COMBINATION 10. Saxes in soli. Trumpets and trombones in background as described above.

Finally, any instrument or instruments may be featured on solo with the background supplied by other different tone colors. The baritone sax (in ensemble) may be taken from the saxes and placed upon the bass line quasi bassoon or on any of the treatments so far written.

ODD COMBINATIONS

As an arranger one does not always arrange for big bands. There are times when you will have to write for flutes and trumpets, trombones and tenors, 1 trumpet, 1 trombone, 2 tenors, 1 baritone, etc. These odd combos are sometimes forced upon the arranger due to the lack of money to hire other musicians or perhaps no other musicians are available. There are also jazz, bosa nova and rhythm and blues combos that are made up of odd combinations because that is the sound desired.

Ex. 20 shows a few different ways to blend and voice these small combos. Ex. 20 Ⓐ: 2 flutes or 2 clarinets with 2 trumpets in cup or stright mutes playing duet. Ⓑ: The same combo but in "4 Way" harmony and they can be dove-tailed. Ⓒ: 2 trombones, 2 tenors and baritone. The tenors and trombones can be dove-tailed. Ⓓ: 2 trumpets, 1 trombone, tenor and baritone. The trumpets and trombone could be in Hat which is a good sound.

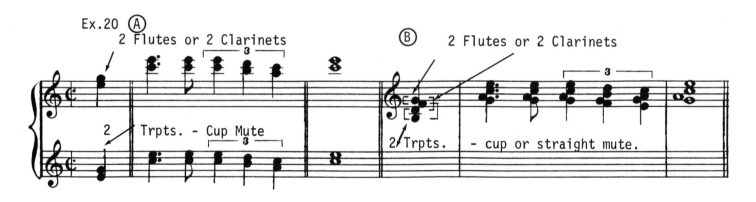

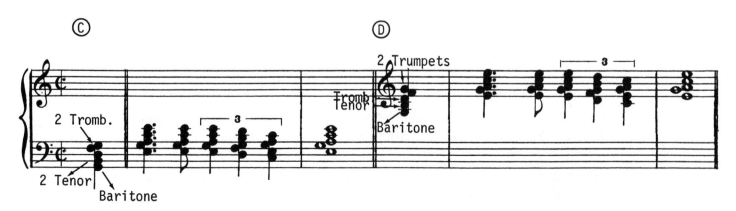

In writing rhythm and blues arrangements, you may use only 2 trumpets, 1 trombone, tenor and baritone. This combo gives a nice full effect with drums and guitar playing a heavy back beat while the bass (which is usually an electric bass) plays a very strong bass line (Ex. 21Ⓐ). Ⓑ shows the type of background that would be played while a blues singer sings the melody.

FREE JAZZ

Until now I have insisted that there should be no parallel perfect 4ths and 5ths when only two voices are in use, but in today's jazz, the musician is constantly fighting for new ways to express himself. The result is that he breaks all of the rules in music. Free jazz is the most modern of the new sounds. Parallel 4ths and 5ths, octaves, weird chord runs with the use of two tonics, one tonic plays chord structure and six semi-tones away the soloist plays the melody. This type of jazz has no set formula, the musicians may play an introductory chorus of 12, 16, 32 or any number of measures, then each soloist plays what he feels. The rhythm section plays a background which enfolds all of the different types of rhythm that have been used in America, such as mambo, montuna, Afro-Cuban. With this type of background, the drums, piano and bass play one altered chord such as G7b, 5b9 for the whole composition, while each soloist in his turn plays just what he feels like playing. However, with close analysis you will find that most of the backgrounds are based on some type of distorted blues progression. The blues play a very important part in all types of jazz. Often, the rhythm section plays 12/8 time with a heavy back beat which is very close to rock 'n roll or rhythm and blues, but the chord structures are much more complex and the solos are pure jazz (Ex. 22Ⓐ). Ⓑ shows this type of jazz using two tenors and rhythm section.

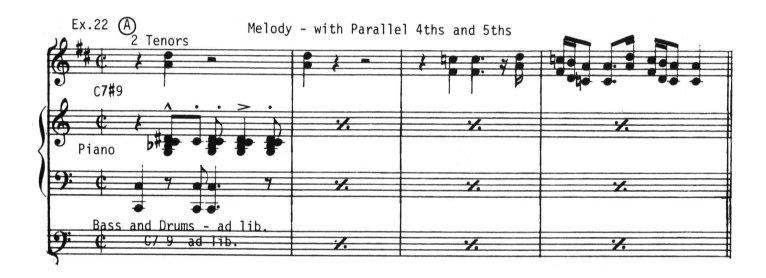

Ex.22 Ⓐ   Melody - with Parallel 4ths and 5ths

CONTRAPUNTAL TREATMENT

Ex. 23 A shows the lead (melody) with counterpoint 1 in the line below; the lowest line has been assigned to counterpoint 2.

Ex. 23 Ⓑ: In the arrangement an interesting treatment and of good sonority has been put into operation. The analysis is: The altos, tenors and baritone are playing C.P.1 in octaves. Trumpet 1 is playing the lead while trumpet 2 and 3 are completing the three part harmony. Trombones 1, 2 and 3 are playing three part harmony on C.P.2.

Part VIII

THE STRINGS WITH BIG BANDS

The violins are sub-divided into three parts—Violin A—Violin B—and Violin C. These, with the viola and cello are used as the string group or section. The string bass may be considered as being a member of the rhythm section and need not be considered in any of the adjustments that are necessary for the string section. Again, there is often only one player to each part and, unless otherwise noted, this will be the working outline as used in the following set-ups. By the way, a part for Violin D is sometimes included. This need not cause any interference in the laying out of the section because the Violin D may, according to the arrangers judgment, double the Violin A at the unison or play the Violin A part an octave lower.

STRINGS AS SOLO, SOLI (Melody or Counter-melody)

1. All strings in direct unison.
2. Violins A , B and C in direct unison; viola and cello in unison an octave lower playing the same music.
3. Violins in unison; viola an octave lower; cello an octave lower than viola.
4. Violins A, B and C in trio harmony; viola and cello in unison an octave lower than Violin A.
5. Violins A, B and C in trio harmony; viola an octave lower than Violin A; cello an octave lower than viola.
6. Violins in trio harmony; viola an octave lower than Violin A; cello on countermelody.
7. Violins A and B in duet; Violin C and viola in same duet but an octave lower; cello on Violin C part an octave lower.
8. Violins and viola parts as in No. 7; cello on counter-melody.
9. Violin A solo; other strings in sustained harmony as background in open voicing or in close voicing.
10. Viola solo; other strings in sustained harmony.
11. Cello solo; other strings in sustained harmony.
12. Violins A, B and C and viola in four-part harmony, in close voicing; cello on Violin A part an octave lower.
13. The treatment of No. 12 may be used with viola on melody and others in four-part harmony as:

```
          ┌ Violin A (Melody)
          │ Violin B
Harmony   │ Violin C
          └ Viola
            Cello (Melody—octave lower)
```

14. As in No. 12, i.e., with the Violin A, B and C and the viola in four-part harmony; cello treated as an independent part on countermelody.
15. Violin A and B in duet; Violin C on Violin A part an octave lower; viola and cello complete the four-part harmony:

```
        ┌ Violin A (Melody)
Duet    └ Violin B
          Violin C (Melody—octave lower)
          Viola
          Cello
```

STRINGS AND SAXOPHONES, CLARINETS, FLUTES, ETC.

When the saxes have solo, soli or counterpoint, the strings may be combined with them as follows:

16. All strings in direct unison with the 1st Alto sax.

17. Violins A, B and C in unison with the 1st Alto sax; viola and cello on same notes in unison an octave lower.

18. Violins A, B and C in unison an octave higher than 1st Alto sax; viola and cello an octave lower in unison.

Clarinet above the staff is not good with Violin (unison) but low clarinets in unison with low strings are suggested.

Strings are good as background to *any solo instrument*—cantabile or swing.

Strings plus Trumpet (open) *unison* are not a good blend, but string plus trumpet *muted* unison are.

Strings (8va) and woodwind and brass produce a full, rich blend (excellent).

Violins (8va) higher than trumpet are in their normal register for ensemble.

The violins may be added to the background for saxes; but with brass as background, use strings independently.

Pizzacato strings add punch (dynamics) to the brass when the brass is playing staccato. Also with piano bells. However, no swing passages for strings.

19. The Sax section in harmony; the strings play the same notes in unison as:

Harmony		
1st Alto Sax	Violin A	Unison with Sax
3rd Alto Sax	Violin B	" " "
2nd Tenor Sax	Violin C	" " "
4th Tenor Sax	Viola	" " "
5th Sax Baritone	Cello	" " "

20. Same as No. 19 but with Violins A, B and C an octave higher than 1st sax, 3rd sax and 2nd tenor sax; viola and cello in unison with 4th tenor sax and baritone as in No. 19.

EFFECTS

Ex. 24 shows some of the effects that have been used by the big bands.

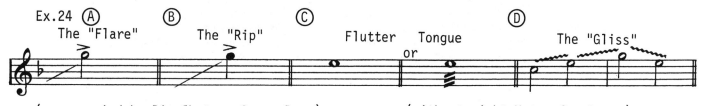

(accompanied by Rim Shot on Snare Drum)   (with straight Mutes for Brass)

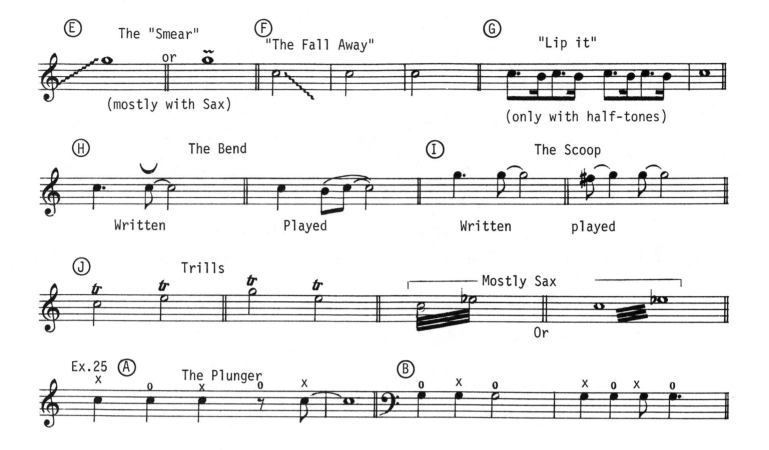

The plunger effect is created by the use of a plunger, the hat or the hand over the bell of the instrument (the saxes are not used for this effect) to get an open and close effect (or+). It is best to keep within the staff when using this effect (Ex. 25).

Part IX

SYMPHONIC EFFECTS IN MODERN ARRANGING

With the use of flutes, the string body, horn in F, the harp and celesta, etc., you can bring to modern music a new world of sound. (Big bands, saxes and rhythm sections are very limited and you must use all kinds of mutes to get effects; even with these you can't reach the higher register.) In the examples that follow you will find many new ways to use the symphony orchestra in modern composition. Analyze each example minutely and make absolutely sure that you understand why each instrument is written as it is. Notice also how completely the music is written. You must not forget that when writing for musicians that are used to playing in symphony orchestras, nothing can be left to the imagination. In a word, *they don't swing,* but if you write exactly what you have in mind, they will play it.

While the symphony orchestra designates the violins as 1 and 2, I mark them A, B, C.

Ex. 26. Violin A, B, C background (muted) viola and cello solo (muted).

Ex. 27. Violin A, B muted playing solo on G string, Violin C, viola and cellos muted playing background.

Ex. 28. 12 Violins playing jazz (a very dynamic sound), violas and cellos pizz. fill-ins, flutes fill-ins and horns in F in solo.

Ex. 29. 12 Violins playing melody on G string. Viola and cello background, flute counter-melody, horns in F background.

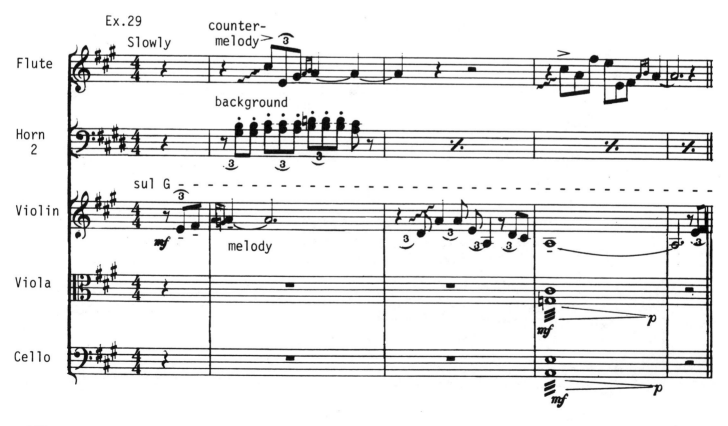

Ex. 30. 12 Violins playing counter-melody. Violas and cellos background, flute solo, horns and brass background with harp playing accompaniment chords, drums and tamborine rhythm, and notice that the timpani is very quietly playing the bass line with the bass, which is a wonderful use of the timpani.

Ex. 31. The string body is divided to play melody and counter-melody. Notice how perfectly balanced they are. Notice also how the use of divisi helps to balance the strings. Here again the timpani is on the bass line with bass plays arco, brass play background. The flute joins in with Violin A in last four measures which gives a still richer and fuller sound.

N.B. When dividing the strings for balance, if there is an odd number always place them on the top melody line. For example, 4 violins playing the melody in three octaves, place 2 violins on top line and one each on the remaining two lines. With 5 violins, playing 4-part harmony, place 2 violins on the top voice and one on each of the remaining voices, etc.

Ex. 32. Violins and violas playing harmonics with tremolo and cello playing bottom notes (the bass would be too heavy). Guitar playing solo in 4th with lowered 7th and 3rd and raised 4th stops of the scale. Harp playing harmonics, tambourine and drums rhythm. This effect is that of rain falling very lightly on a roof. The guitar is playing the blues and the title of this composition is "Raining the Blues."

Extract from The Blues Suite — Mickey Baker

Ex. 33. Again here the strings are divided for balance, reinforced by the celesta in the top octave and the flute an octave lower, timpani and bass on bass-line brass plays the counter-melody while the horns in F sustain background. This gives a very brilliant and thrilling effect.

Part X

CHORAL ARRANGING

The average range for voices in Ex. 1.

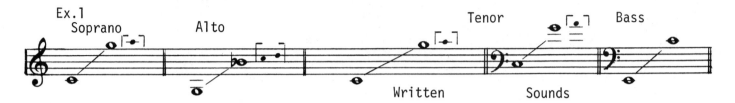

The alto voice should not lie more than an octave from the soprano or tenor voice, but the bass may lie a 10th or 12th below the tenor (Ex. 2 Ⓐ, Ⓑ).

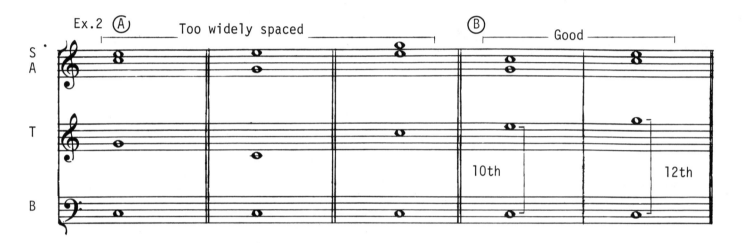

VOICE LEADING

The melody and bass are flexible, but the inner voices are led as smoothly as possible.

When arranging for two voices the best intervals are the 3rds and 6ths. If possible, parallel 4ths and 5ths are to be avoided. Parallel octaves may be used to strengthen an important line.

Parallel 4ths and 5ths are bad only when in two parts. Octaves may be used on any important line.

The melody is usually in the soprano but it can also be in any of the other voices. Hand clapping and humming are effective in background (Ex. 4).

Ex.4

The discant is effective in chord writing. Ex. 5 shows discant in high soprano with S.A.T. singing in harmony while bass sustains bass line.

Ex.5

Ex. 6. Solo voice sings melody, the remaining voices sing rhythmic background.

Ex.6

There are many ways to write for voices, in fact, any of the 4-part voicing for brass or saxes will work out fine with the singing voices, but always in close harmony and bearing in mind the range of the soprano, alto, tenor and bass.

The male quartet employs T.T.B.B. Ex. 7Ⓐ shows the best range for voices. Ⓑ and Ⓒ show voicing.

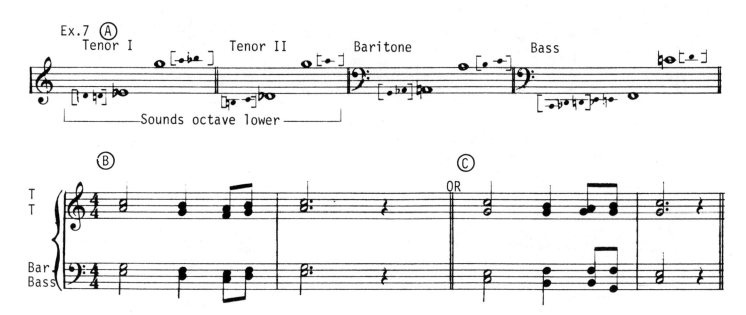

In the old time Barber Shop Quartet style, there are effects that are useful at times. The 2nd tenor usually takes the lead and the parts are named top tenor, lead tenor, baritone and bass. Ex. 8 shows a good voicing of the Barber Shop Quartet.

The Barber Shop effect is strongest at the close of the cadence and here every man is for himself—anything goes—as long as they finally reach the closing chord.

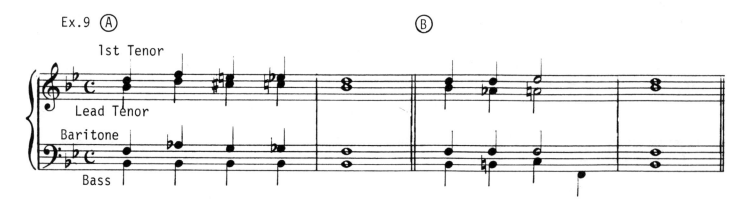

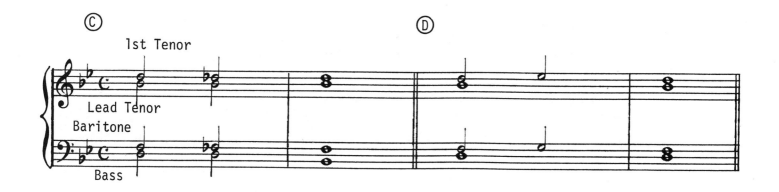

TBB COMBINATION

In this three part male chorus, the parts are sometimes written as, tenor, tenor, bass but it would seem better to name them tenor, baritone and bass. This combination is not as full and rich as TTBB arrangements but it is possible to write fine arrangements for it. The treatment is as with the male quartet. The arrangements for the combination are best used for glee clubs and other such groups and so it is well to reduce the voice range for the different voices as in Ex. 10.

Ex.10   Tenor

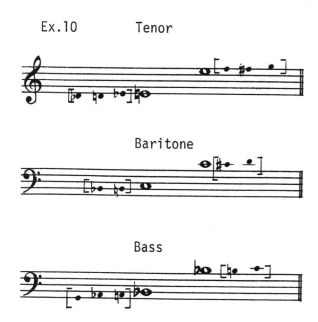

There need not be as much crossing of parts as in the TTBB because there is one part less which causes the harmony to be more "open." When the writing is contrapuntal or canonic, the crossing of parts becomes more in order.

While the barber-shop style of writing is more normal with TTBB, it is possible to offer a semblance of this style with TBB, by following closely the barber shop routines.

TB COMBINATION

When it is desirable to write for two-parts, these voices will provide interesting material. The best range is shown in Ex. 11.

FEMALE VOICES (Treble Voices)

The total range of this combination is small and so there are limitations in writing for it. Also, the tone color is the same and apt to produce a monotonous effect unless a male solo voice can be used. Therefore, the groups are limited to small numbers, unless there can be an interesting orchestral background. But, to obtain variety in mixed voice writing, parts of an arrangement are written for treble voices alone. It is best to have a staff for each part. In writing for all treble it is advisable to extend the range slightly above the normal range.

SSA COMBINATION

These parts are Soprano I, Soprano II and Alto on three staves. (If this combination is to be written for high school groups of boy's voices, label them as "high", "medium" and "low".)

When writing for "8" voices (S.S.A.A.T.T.B.B.) it is possible to have the T.T. B.B. sing the same notes as the S.S. A.A. or consider the S.S. A.A. as trumpets and the T.T. B.B. as saxes or trombones with all of the orchestral devices available.